What Pe

I greatly appreciate Mark's investment in this work and the insights, experiences and wisdom he shares. It's great to see Mark helping others improve their lives, personally and professionally. It's inspiring to me on so many levels.
Dan Bilderback, Talent Leader (Financial Services)

I loved the contention of this book and that Mark speaks directly to the reader as a voice of experience. The metaphor of traffic cop is a perfect illustration of modern-day leader experience, and his cautionary description of how some managers get promoted is spot-on. The investment theme is so clever, an approach any leader can apply.
Kristie Provost-Gorman, Ethics and Compliance Officer

Stakeholders by Mark Englizian is an essential read for anyone looking to truly understand the human dynamics within the ecosystem of business. With decades of experience and insightful observations, Englizian argues that people are not just assets but also the very foundation of any successful organization. This book offers a fresh perspective, breaking down the traditional views and providing a comprehensive framework for making value-based decisions that benefit all stakeholders. It's a must-read for business leaders, managers, and anyone committed to fostering a thriving organizational environment.
Dr. Marshall Goldsmith, *New York Times* bestselling author

The mantra of 'People are our most important asset' is both trite and useless for providing guidance regarding how to effectively lead companies. This book authored by Mark Englizian shifts

the view of people from being objects to human beings with inherent dignity and varied interests no matter where they are in the organization, regardless of how they interact with the organization as customers, suppliers, investors, and in communities. It is a much-needed people-focused approach to leading organizations in the 21st century.
Dr. Patrick Wright, Department Chair, Darla Moore School of Business, University of South Carolina

This was an easy read, very understandable, but full of wisdom that appeals to the intelligent reader. The more I read, the more I wanted to read. My key lesson from this book? Every stakeholder matters.
Randy Fox, Acclaimed Motivational Speaker

This book is enjoyable and thought-provoking, with real-life examples that are both captivating and helpful. Englizian has a knack for story-telling, which is refreshing in this literary genre. The section on leadership really resonated with me, and I agree that maturity is a more helpful construct than EQ.
Stephen Lindemann, Consultant, Executive Coach

Stakeholders fills a critical gap in the business literature, clearly articulating the conflicts and common interests of competing groups in the business eco-system. Englizian perfectly makes the case for why many of the CEOs I advise feel lonely and pressured, as different groups vie for resources. Thankfully, Englizian also lays out concrete methods for executives to navigate stakeholder interests with integrity and help their organizations thrive.
Steve Welch, Board Advisor and CEO Coach

I was very impressed with the thinking, writing skills, and story-telling. Mark Englizian does a masterful job of articulating the two most important aspects of all stakeholders ... They intersect directly or indirectly, and they all coexist in an ecosystem. He does this through story and example of how the best do it. Most importantly, Mark leaves us with the secret sauce (the *what*) to ensure we can help our organizations improve within the context of a leadership ethos (the *how* of mature leadership).

Dr. Mark Blankenship, Former Chief Strategy Officer, SHRM Foundation Board

I very much enjoyed the insights Mark shared from his extraordinary career, as he continues to raise business professionalism to levels not always seen in US corporations. I am savoring Mark's insights, appreciating the logical construct and enjoying his conversational writing style. I heartily agree with Mark's thesis that the strategic importance of stakeholders is inadequately understood and addressed by business leaders. As a former graduate student (Harvard MBA), I can affirm this book presents an excellent outline for a business school course.

Kelly Jensen, Business Consultant, Healthcare Executive

Stakeholders calls on the reader to think deeply about a diverse and broader array of people with a vested interest in a business, not just shareholders. In Mark's love of metaphors, he astutely takes the reader through a case-study learning that illustrates successes and challenges with well-known companies. It's a powerful way to breathe life into his salient leadership points while allowing you to challenge your own thinking. He thoughtfully examines his own career journey and his growth in valuing diverse stakeholders and the importance of mature leadership.

Val Rupp, Technology Leader

Many understand the importance of people in making a business successful, but few see the entire ecosystem and the various

intersections in its totality. Englizian does a marvelous job of helping the reader think like the most successful entrepreneurs and business executives by providing insight into business operations and financials, along with leveraging the people that make up the critical audiences a business relies on. While many CEOs espouse that people are their most important asset, this book goes well beyond employees in showcasing how true that statement really is.
Kevin Oakes, CEO and Entrepreneur

I love the total stakeholder management focus of Englizian's book. It takes the long-standing mantra/promise of 'stakeholder capitalism' and gives concrete examples of what it looks like, and why it matters to the enterprise and its broader ecosystem. I also appreciate the simplicity of the secret sauce. This approach to macro-level systems thinking and eco-system well-being is often blocked by short-term pressures (notably quarterly financial guidance and related financial incentives) and lack of long-term vision for how the enterprise must evolve to continue to prosper.
Kevin Martin, Business Research Executive

This book will help you understand and effectively harness your stakeholder ecosystem. Mark Englizian's career spans over three decades of HR executive roles at exemplary companies including Microsoft, Amazon, and Walgreens. That's impressive, but even more impressive is his ability to distill those experiences into a unique, coherent, understandable and actionable framework, with the stakeholder ecosystem at its core.
Dr. John Boudreau, Professor Emeritus, Marshall School of Business, University of Southern California

Stakeholders is a fascinating book with a refreshing and challenging perspective on the importance of the people who make businesses a success (or failure). Using an in-depth and compelling case study, a variety of business examples and Mark's personal stories, this book draws the reader in and keeps them engaged. Regardless of which stakeholder group you're in (or thinking about), the concepts Mark presents will challenge your assumptions, your beliefs and, hopefully, your behaviors as you relate and connect with others. I found *Stakeholders* to be un-put-down-able!

Linda Miller, Master Certified Coach

STAKEHOLDERS

The Intersection of Human Beings in the
Eco-System of Business

STAKEHOLDERS

The Intersection of Human Beings in the
Eco-System of Business

Foreword by Marshall Goldsmith

Mark Englizian

BUSINESS
BOOKS

London, UK
Washington, DC, USA

CollectiveInk

First published by Business Books, 2025
Business Books is an imprint of Collective Ink Ltd.,
Unit 11, Shepperton House, 89 Shepperton Road, London, N1 3DF
office@collectiveink.com
www.collectiveink.com
www.collectiveink.com/business-books

For distributor details and how to order please visit the 'Ordering' section on our website.

Text copyright: Mark Englizian 2024

ISBN: 978 1 80341 909 1
978 1 80341 912 1 (ebook)
Library of Congress Control Number: 2024913975

All rights reserved. Except for brief quotations in critical articles or reviews, no part of this book may be reproduced in any manner without prior written permission from the publishers.

The rights of Mark Englizian as author have been asserted in accordance with the Copyright, Designs and Patents Act 1988.

A CIP catalogue record for this book is available from the British Library.

Design: Lapiz Digital Services

UK: Printed and bound by CPI Group (UK) Ltd, Croydon, CR0 4YY
Printed in North America by CPI GPS partners

We operate a distinctive and ethical publishing philosophy in all areas of our business, from our global network of authors to production and worldwide distribution.

TABLE OF CONTENTS

FOREWORD by Marshall Goldsmith xiii

SECTION ONE xv

Introduction xvii
Chapter One: Case Study 5
Chapter Two: Money Matters 11

SECTION TWO 19

Chapter Three: People Groups 21
Chapter Four: Competing Interests 39
Chapter Five: Survive and Thrive 57
Chapter Six: Intersection Chaos 67

SECTION THREE 75

Chapter Seven: Priorities 77
Chapter Eight: Affordability of Investing in People 85
Chapter Nine: Repurposing Legacy Investments 93
Chapter Ten: Modernizing for Asset Efficiency 101
Chapter Eleven: Use It or Lose It 105

SECTION FOUR 111

Chapter Twelve: Decision Time 113
Chapter Thirteen: The Sauce 127
Chapter Fourteen: A New Personal Ethos 139
Author Notes and Acknowledgements 145
Citations and Sources 155

This volume is dedicated to my four adult children, Jennifer, Matthew, Brianna and Chelsea, whom I deeply love and respect. You are the next generation of business leaders, and you give me hope.

FOREWORD

In a world where business success is often measured by profit margins and shareholder returns, Mark Englizian's *Stakeholders* provides a refreshing and necessary shift in perspective. The essence of this book is simple yet profound: people are not just assets to be managed, but the very lifeblood of any organization. Englizian draws from his vast experience to highlight the importance of understanding and valuing every individual within the business ecosystem, from front-line workers, to executives, and beyond. His insights are a call to action for leaders to rethink how they engage with and invest in their people.

Englizian's deep dive into the dynamics of business relationships is both enlightening and practical. He explores the often-overlooked complexities of human interactions within a corporate setting, shedding light on how these relationships can make or break a company. By emphasizing the importance of empathy, respect, and mutual benefit, Englizian challenges us to move beyond the traditional, transactional approach to business. Instead, he advocates for a more holistic view that recognizes the diverse contributions of all stakeholders.

The strength of *Stakeholders* lies in its ability to translate theory into actionable strategies. Englizian provides readers with a clear framework for making decisions that are not only ethically sound but also strategically advantageous. His approach is grounded in real-world examples and backed by solid research, making it a practical guide for leaders at all levels. Whether you're a seasoned executive or just starting your career, this book offers valuable lessons on how to create a more inclusive and effective organization.

What sets this book apart is Englizian's candid and personal storytelling. He shares his own experiences and observations, giving readers a glimpse into his journey and the lessons he has learned along the way. This personal touch not only makes the content more relatable, but also underscores the authenticity of his message. Englizian's passion for people and his commitment to fostering positive change in the business world shine through on every page.

Englizian has crafted a compelling manifesto for a more humane and sustainable approach to business. This book is a testament to the power of putting people first and a guide for anyone who wants to build a thriving, resilient organization. As you read through these pages, I hope you are inspired to rethink your own approach to leadership and to embrace the transformative potential of truly valuing your stakeholders.

Dr. Marshall Goldsmith is the *Thinkers50 #1* Executive Coach and New York Times bestselling author of *The Earned Life, Triggers,* and *What Got You Here Won't Get You There.*

SECTION ONE

Author's Objective: **Introduce** *the reader to the big picture of people in business and why excellence in this area matters.*

Introduction

> *Sustainable profits are the successful outcome of organizations that are mission driven and focus on all their stakeholders. In the future, every company will need to focus on its purpose in order to establish legitimacy in serving society by creating value for all stakeholders. (Bill George, former CEO Medtronic, Senior Fellow at Harvard Business School and author of "Discover Your True North.")*[1]

Thousands of books have been written about "business." Among the millions of books (on all subjects) available for purchase on Amazon, there are 21 categories in the Business and Money section — each with hundreds or even thousands of titles available. A different website promises to give a reader free access to 250 books on business! Media outlets give prospective readers curated advice on the best business books released in any given year. Suffice it to say, the market for books on business appears to be quite mature and well-supplied.

So, why write one more book about business? Let me answer that question with another: "of the business books that you have read in the past five years, how many focused on the 'people side' of business"? Sure, there are stories about great companies and successful leaders who are willing to share what they did well (and not so well). Meanwhile, other books claim to reveal best practices for finding, rewarding, developing, and promoting great talent (people) for the good of the company. These types of books can be helpful, but they don't provide a full picture of the people's side of business. **In this book, we are exploring new territory.**

It is possible that you work for a company that publicly states something like "people are our greatest asset." This is not uncommon. But honestly, because the actual meaning behind this statement varies from one employer to the next, its impact is underwhelming. For one thing, the reference to "people" is almost always a reference only to their employees (and fails to acknowledge other people groups essential to a functioning business). Referring to employees at Company A, this means "come work for us, and we will treat you fairly." At Company B, it is an acknowledgement that human beings are necessary to run a big company "and we have many of them, so in the sense of volume they are an asset that cannot be ignored." At Company C, it may mean that "we pay attention to employees and invest in them with a higher priority than even our customers." (The theory behind this thinking is that happy employees do the best job of keeping customers happy too.) Or finally, at Company D, it could mean that they value the legacy and culture to such a large degree that they have purposefully given ownership of the company to their employees. This could be in the form of an employee stock ownership arrangement, or concentrating share ownership to a small group of family members or legacy owners who can be trusted with an asset of this magnitude.

I get all that, and those approaches can be valuable. But for me, the statement about "people being the greatest asset" has been diluted, mis-represented, falsified, and downright betrayed in countless environments by many companies. From my experience in business over the past four decades, I have come to realize that the statement has very little meaning anymore.

Now, you may be wondering why I am critical of a commonly held belief that you would expect a human resources leader to champion. See, my issue is not in the acknowledgement of the value of people to an organization. My issue is with the unthinking degradation of human beings as "assets." I do believe strongly in the roles human beings play in the world of business, and in making performance assessments about the contributions of people in the proper context.

Putting aside our discussion about that specific statement, I believe that the operation of business and the contributions of people are inextricably linked. You cannot have one without the other. **A business without people** is at best a product that sells itself and is transacted virtually, using technology in a "set-it-and-forget" mode — it only works in a very small number of cases. **People without a business** are a collection of like-minded individuals (like a book club, perhaps) who come together for reasons unrelated to products, customers, buying, selling, and creating profits — not a bad reality, but not a business.

Taking this one step further, when you combine a business with the human factor, "the contributions of people" is a multi-faceted and diverse picture more complex than you might imagine. When most of us think of "people in business," we immediately think of employees. Not incorrect, but certainly incomplete. In fact, the people who engage with the typical for-profit, publicly or privately-owned company in business are quite extensive in number. Take employees for example, who are certainly important, but you would be hard pressed to find a company where executives, people managers and front-line workers all have the exact same goals, expectations, and priorities. Therefore, we must admit that the term "employees" is a diverse population of human beings to be studied in the context of the other human stakeholders, for reasons that will become obvious.

In addition to the employees — who are executives, people managers, and front-line workers — other people including shareholders, investors, customers, labor unions, suppliers, partners, distributors, third-party sellers, regulators, watchdogs, activists, elected officials and the business media are critical to the existence of any business. These categories of people have their own backgrounds, experiences, ideas, feedback, agendas, definitions of success, and above all, competing expectations — all the while seeking to exert their unique brand of influence on the direction of your business.

Let's look at two examples to fully understand what I mean. Stated plainly, **executives** are typecast for being talented, experienced, and consumed by self-interest. This certainly doesn't describe 100% of executives, but let's not argue the point since we plan to study this population in greater detail later in the book. On the other hand, **front-line workers** are lower on the totem pole in status and pay, living paycheck to paycheck and rarely getting an opportunity to share their ideas for improving the business. Two people groups, subsets of what we call "employees," and yet they could not be more different in composition and influence.

Making the point again with another population of people — shareholders. This group of human beings is made up of elected board members, executives, professional investors, wealth fund managers, public and private institutions, day traders, cause activists, individuals from the public and rank and file employees (in many cases), all of whom buy into the story of your business in one way or another. These people have one thing in common (share ownership), but very little else. Their purpose, agenda, assessment of the present, and vision for the future of your company could not be more different.

Here is the primary contention of this book. The people who reside in the eco-system of business are more in number and diverse in perspective than is usually understood, discussed in business school, or written about in the hundreds of books available to you as the reader. It is foolhardy to believe an executive or any business leader can ignore or work around any one of these people groups who possess power and influence over the business and the company. It is up to you as

supervisors, managers, executives, and outside directors to set priorities and make value-based decisions that constructively benefit all the stakeholder groups engaged and invested in your business.

People are essential; they are critical and foundational to the success of your business. You make decisions every day that impact not only your employees, but also the diverse populations of people who have taken up residence on the periphery of your company. This book will help you see the "big picture of people," bring clarity to what people want, provide a framework for evaluating priorities, and give you confidence that you are making the best investment decisions for the present and future health of your company.

The intended audience for this book is generally anyone interested in business, and more specifically the businessperson interested in learning new things and testing cutting-edge ideas. You could be a business school or executive education student, a people manager, team leader, executive, elected director, or investor. (You will find references to these roles throughout the book.) What you all have in common is a desire to keep learning and growing professionally.

The format of this book is divided into four sections that focus on these action words: (1) introduce; (2) identify; (3) equip; and (4) commission. The title page of each section briefly describes what you can expect. And the opening page of each chapter begins with a true-life anecdote or illustration that is meant to stir your appetite for the content that follows, sometimes by introducing a little controversy. The use of a particular anecdote or illustration (in this manner) should not be interpreted as an endorsement of any company, business practice, or public figure.

There is one more important declaration I need to make before we get started. The content you will read is sourced primarily from my own personal life history, my experiences in business over parts of four decades, and observations that represent what I have seen and heard from thousands of encounters with people from all walks of life. It has never been my objective to secure consensus from readers because my experience is what it is — a telling of my co-existence with people in business — from my own perspective. My guess is that you will resonate positively from most of what you read here. However, there is a possibility you will discover pieces of content that appear to be controversial, or possibly contrary to your own point of view or experience. If the intersection of your view, and mine, causes you to think harder and more comprehensively about how people intersect in the eco-system of business, then I will consider that to be a resounding success.

Chapter One:

Case Study

During my decade as dean of Harvard Business School, I spent hundreds of hours talking with our alumni. To enliven these conversations, I relied on a favorite question: "What was the most important thing you learned from your time in our MBA program?"
Responses varied, but most often alumni highlighted a personal quality or skill like "increased self-confidence" or "the ability to advocate for a point of view' or 'knowing how to work closely with others to solve problems." And when I asked how they developed these capabilities, they inevitably mentioned the magic of the case method. (Nitin Nohria)[1]

Welcome to case study learning. I was first attracted to case study learning when I was recruited to help review and evaluate content submitted to Harvard Business Press. The opportunities for learning within the Harvard system were compelling, particularly for someone who pursued business education mid-career, rather than at the front-end. The Harvard case studies prepare readers "to navigate business challenges by immersion in real-world scenarios."[2] Not content with traditional education where concepts are theoretical and without context, these case studies are written by Harvard professors and other renowned business educators to bring a sense of realism into the "classroom" environment. Case studies are known to promote retention and comprehension. After all, who doesn't like a good story?

Inspired by this approach, we begin this book with a case study of our own. It's essential that we choose a company story that adequately depicts the "big picture" of the people side of business. There are literally tens of thousands of stories in the world of business. One way to sort through all the potential learnings is to look at the Fortune 500, the magazine's list of the top 500 US companies (based on annual revenue). Another possible source is the Standard & Poor's (S&P) 500, which is a stock market index tracking the largest publicly traded US companies according to their market valuation, or "market cap" (number of outstanding shares X fair market value).

However, focusing on one specific company will limit our study because there is only so much information we can ascertain from public documents. Therefore, as a work-around we have created a fictitious company that is a composite of what we see in the largest US for-profit organizations, combined with my own experiences at Fortune 500 companies — both as an employee leader and, later in my career, as an advisor to boards of directors and executive teams.

Let's begin.

Our fictitious case study company was founded in 1982 in DeKalb, Illinois, with the opening of its first store known locally as Hanson's Home & Hardware. Ted Hanson was well into his career as an accomplished firefighter, raising four sons with his wife, Peggy. Ted was gifted in all things mechanical, building much of their first family home, repairing his own vehicles, and always available when called upon to help friends and neighbors with their home maintenance and do-it-yourself projects. Because of the traditional but unusual work schedule of the firefighter (24 hours on-duty, 48 hours off-duty), Ted enjoyed working around the house and engaging with four active sons on his days off. Always thinking, Ted had a new business idea that he thought was worth exploring. Regarding the origins of the company, his son Cliff recalled his dad saying, "instead of making multiple trips to the hardware store, the paint store, the lumber yard, and the garden center to get all the supplies for my home project, it occurred to me and Peggy that customers would like having all these items available under one roof, sort of a one-stop shopping experience for the do-it-yourselfer." And there you have it, Hanson's Home & Hardware was born and continued to grow moderately over the next few years.

Customers did like the idea of having all these supplies under one roof, and Ted and his small team of employees liked being able to say to customers, "yes, we've got that." It took some trial and error to inventory the store appropriately, to price items competitively, recruit and train employees and expand into more small cities. The store expansion strategy was intentional, targeting markets with a population between 10,000 and 30,000 people. The thinking was that the market opportunity needed to be large enough to justify the amount of inventory they typically carried, and not too large to attract the big-box home improvement retailers who would dominate the market and make it difficult for the Hansons to compete. As the company grew to over 25 locations, Ted became president and CEO of the newly named corporation, HomeSource, Inc. Store managers were identified from his growing number of trusted employees, and from his sons who had come of age and began to actively participate in management of the business.

Fast forward a couple of decades, when the HomeSource company grew their retail footprint to over 390 small market locations primarily in the midwestern states, plus Kentucky, Tennessee, Florida and the mountain west region of Montana, Wyoming, Colorado, Utah, and Arizona. Born out of necessity, the market analytics function became its own profitable division, as did a land management division providing forestry products directly to the stores. Depending on market size and other local economic factors, some of the locations grew beyond the initial standard 8000 square foot building envelope to accommodate additional customer needs for gardening supplies, outdoor living accessories, equine products, and equipment rentals.

The impact of Hanson's success on the local community of DeKalb was significant. At its peak, Hanson's payroll included nearly 500 employees in DeKalb, with some jobs in the stores and other jobs at headquarters. These employment opportunities were linked to middle and upper middle-income lifestyles, all of which contributed to local tax revenue, economic growth, volunteering, and talent in the community. One former Hanson's store manager ran for mayor, another served two terms on the City Council, and another became chaplain of the DeKalb Fire Department. To preserve the quality of life in their community, schools and playgrounds were built, churches multiplied, college enrollment increased, philanthropic donations ticked up and the economy remained strong as new housing developments accommodated population growth.

About 30 years after the launch of Hanson's, a private equity (PE) firm approached Ted and his family about selling the company. With each store averaging $7 million in annual sales, plus the licensing and consulting income from the market analytics group and royalties from forestry sales, the HomeSource company was generating over $3 billion in total annual revenues and about $150 million in annual EBITDA (earnings before interest, taxes, depreciation, and amortization). The PE firm offered to buy out the Hanson family and other long-term investors who owned shares of the company, creating a once-in-a-lifetime liquidity event for the family/investor ownership group. The PE firm was very clear that they wanted to retain the family legacy and culture of the company, retain key employees, and bring new investment to the store experience for customers. Once the proposed sale had been completed, the PE firm also pledged to give HomeSource access to their best subject matter experts in the areas of financial controls and reporting, IT infrastructure, supply chain, revenue management, and human resources.

In 2014, the Hansons sold their company to the PE firm for $1.9 billion, not including debt. After paying off their creditors, settling with investors, paying out stock option gains for executives and key employees, and establishing a family foundation to support charitable causes, each member of the Hanson founding family was richly rewarded for a lifetime of hard work and dedication to the business. The PE firm gradually brought in a new executive team and followed through on their investment commitments. The business continued to grow profitably until 2023 when ownership in the HomeSource company was made available through an Initial Public Offering, with JP Morgan as the investment adviser. With 100 million shares outstanding at an offering price of $30, the new public entity of HomeSource Inc. was valued at $3 billion. The PE firm did very well, making good on its buyout investment of the Hansons' company, and accumulating over $5 billion in earnings and appreciation over the ten years of ownership.

The company currently has over 32,000 employees deployed in over 500 locations, generating annual revenues of $7.2 billion and $800 million in EBITDA. Since inception, investor/owners of shares in the HomeSource public company have experienced valuation increases that significantly exceed returns when compared to the broader capital market indices.

Chapter Two:

Money Matters

Business is an art as well as a science. It's a matter of practical experience, judgment, foresight and luck. To be successful in business, you must master the basics of business success.
There are three major reasons why businesses fail: lack of money, lack of knowledge and lack of support. By mastering the basics of business success, you'll gain the knowledge necessary to acquire the support and money you need for your business. (Entrepreneur, Brian Tracy)[1]

Now that we have an overview of the case study, it is critical to the theme of this book that you deeply understand the people groups who influence and reside within the eco-system of business, so you can confidently engage with them and deliver results for your company. But before we go there, it is always appropriate in a conversation about business to ask and answer this question: "so, how do we make money around here?" Let's agree that regardless of your role in the business enterprise, it is critical that you deeply understand the answer to that question for the business and industry you are in. An organization dedicated to making a difference in the marketplace trades in two fundamental currencies: human effort, and money. Here are some financial concepts that are critical to this exchange, accompanied by some examples that reveal different applications of these concepts by industry.

Annual Revenues: The simplest way of thinking about revenue is the money a business receives from selling a product or service. A transaction occurs and money changes hands. Your cash register (in the formative days at Hanson's Home & Hardware), Point of Sale system (POS) or credit card account records the transaction, reducing your inventory as items are purchased and increasing your cash or bank account with the dollar amount you have assigned to that item. The revenue you receive is a function of demand, price, and customer loyalty.

The volume of revenues generated from business activity is the defining limitation on hundreds of decisions you will make as an owner or manager. I once overheard an operations leader say in a weekly business review, "revenue covers a multitude of sins." However, the details of how revenue is generated profoundly matter. Think of revenue as the multiplication of price and units sold, like in the case of the Chipotle quick service restaurant chain where the price of a burrito bowl and a beverage is around $15. The company reported 2023 annual revenue of approximately $10 billion, now that's a lot of burritos — over 650 million! Stating the obvious, no single Chipotle location can churn out that kind of volume, which is why they need 3400 restaurants and 115,000 employees to generate such impressive revenue.

In contrast, take for example the Porsche company who designs and manufactures luxury vehicles with an average suggested retail price of $150,000 per unit that generates over $40 billion in annual revenue. The math leads me to presume Porsche produces about 275,000 vehicles for consumption, primarily in two German manufacturing plants (Stuttgart and Leipzig) that employ about 32,000 people.

Comparing these two successful companies "apples-to-apples" (to the extent possible), Chipotle generates $10 billion of revenue by selling 650 million units, whereas Porsche generates a $10 billion revenue run rate by selling 68,000 units. Why does this matter? Because how your company generates revenue (price x units) is critically important to how you make money, where you are located, how many people you employ and the quality and quantity of stakeholders who engage with your company.

Cost of Goods Sold: Whatever you sell, whether a product or a service, you will incur an acquisition cost to bring it into your inventory. Cost of Goods Sold (COGS) is an important line item on your financial statements because it is immediately subtracted from your revenues. You may be the manufacturer of the items you sell, or you have a purchasing agreement with the manufacturer that fixes the price you will pay for a duration of time. In some cases, there is a "middleman" or distributor who warehouses thousands of items from multiple manufacturers and ships them to the customer-facing retailer when the store inventory runs low. Regardless of the arrangement for securing inventory, the business incurs a cash cost.

The cost of goods story at Microsoft is compelling due to the unique nature of how products are designed, built and sold to customers. Computer software is a derivative of human intelligence, meaning the primary raw material needed are people trained to write code and turn it into commands that operate the many forms of technology so commonplace today. In this case, inventory and employees (doing the work of software development) are one and the same. And because the cost of labor is typically noted in another category Selling, General and Administration accounted for after the calculation of gross profit, the software development cost of goods is nearly $0 and the gross profit generated approaches 100% of revenue. (Note: some of you may be wondering about the cost to build the computer, including hardware design, silicon wafer chips, graphical interface, etc. Those are costs absorbed by the computer manufacturer, not Microsoft which primarily is in the software business.) Therefore, the industry you are in, the business model you operate, and where your revenue dollars flow has an incredible influence on your business and the role stakeholders play in the success of your company.

Gross Profit: At this point in our understanding of money matters, we know two things. (A) how much revenue we bring in from selling stuff; and (B) how much it costs to buy that stuff from suppliers and bring it into inventory. Gross profit is the arithmetic of subtracting (B) from (A). If you bring in $100 of revenue, and subtract $50 for COGS, you have a gross profit of $50 or a gross profit margin of 50%. Does your instinct tell you that looks like good business performance? Your answer could be, "that depends".

We will see later that technology companies currently dominate the list of the world's most valuable companies, and this "anomaly" of gross profit at 80–100% of revenue is one of the most significant contributing factors. If you are a business owner or investor, are you likely to be satisfied with a gross profit margin of 50%? To help you better answer that question, we need to take a closer look at employee wages, benefits, administrative cost, taxes due, interest on debt, and so much more.

Selling, General & Administration: This cost, known commonly as SG&A expenses, is a large bucket of services that your company pays for — think of it as "the cost of being in business." The largest SG&A expense is typically the wages, benefits, and payroll taxes you pay for the privilege of employing talented people to get all the work done. Other expenses include the professional services provided to the company by accountants, external auditors, attorneys, and recruiting firms. The cost of building rents, utilities, technology licenses, travel and other reasonable business expenses are also typically included in

SG&A costs. Without question, this category of expenditure will quickly shrink your gross margin, maybe even to single digits (in the example of our case study company). However, in a different company and industry, COGS, gross profit/margin, and SG&A expenses could look significantly different than our case study company.

If you study the architecture of jobs in the US economy, the skillsets needed to perform those jobs and the prevailing wages earned by employees with those skills, you will immediately notice how this impacts your SG&A costs. For example:

- If you own or operate a professional dental practice, your most common jobs are hygienists, dental assistants, insurance billing staff, office managers, and receptionists. The average salary for this small team of employees is $60,000 per year.
- If you own or manage an IT security business, your most common jobs are software engineers, database administrators, systems analysts, AI designers, and cybersecurity specialists with a blended average salary of $150,000 per year.

The learning takeaway is that not all jobs are created equal, and a headcount of 1000 in one company means profitability while a headcount of 1000 in another company means insolvency. SG&A costs need to be customized to your business. Your knowledge and understanding of how SG&A expenses impact your specific business is very important to achieving profitability.

Net Profit: This calculation is simply subtracting SG&A expenses from gross profit. In percentage terms, it is known as net margin or operating margin. The importance of operating margin shows up in two ways: (1) management is directly responsible and accountable for everything on this line and above; and (2) net profit needs to be a positive dollar amount since there are some key expenses yet to be paid by the company, such as state and federal taxes and interest on debt (over which management has less influence).

Net Income: If you are the owner, this is the bottom line of the business. After everything gets paid, this is how much remains for business expansion, cash reserves, and dividends to share owners. So now, let's go back to that question we asked about gross margin and apply it to the amount of net income you see on your company's income statement. Does this amount give you the opportunity to invest in what you need to sustain and grow the business? If not, you will need to explore alternatives such as raising prices (e.g. Nordstrom, where customers may be willing to absorb price increases), finding suppliers who will provide quantity discounts (e.g. Walmart, who has mastered negotiating with suppliers), minimizing your administrative expenses (e.g. Amazon, known for keeping internal costs low so it can pass the savings along to customers), employing an abundance of front-line employees (e.g. McDonalds, employer to millions of lower paid entry-level workers), or moving your business to a more cost effective, tax friendly location (e.g. Tesla, who moved its manufacturing plants from California to Texas).

Income Statement: The items described in the paragraphs above are found on the "Income Statement," which is the most frequently reviewed financial document in business. Here is what it looked like for the HomeSource Corporation in fiscal year 2013, just prior to the sale of the business to a private equity firm. Net income of $150 million seems like a lot of money, until you realize that planned expansion into new markets with more inventory, store conversions, format remodeling and investment in a management training institute will exhaust most of these cash reserves.

HOMESOURCE CORPORATION	FY 2013
Total Revenue	$ 3,147,983,100
Cost of Goods Sold	$ (1,858,012,500)
Gross Profit	$ 1,289,970,600
Gross Profit Margin	41%
SG&A Expenses	$ (1,025,844,900)
Net Profit	$ 264,125,700
Net Profit Margin	8%
Taxes, Interest & Other	$ (113,687,200)
Net Income	$ 150,438,500
Net Income Margin	5%

Economic Versus Accounting Cost: I learned this difference from my CEO. We were having an email conversation on the topic of employee time-off. I researched what we were offering and compared it to market norms for our industry. I had conducted employee forums to get feedback directly from workers. I had connected with HR business partners and people managers who typically heard uncensored opinions on what concerned people on their teams. Based on my research, and my (then) 15 years of experience managing people issues in the workplace, I offered up a proposal to increase the value of our paid time-off policies. After some going back and forth, I figured this would probably require a face-to-face meeting to get a resolution — until he asked me this unexpected question: "will the policy change result in economic cost or accounting cost?" He was asking whether the income statement and cash flow would be impacted (examples would be writing a check to purchase training manuals, or funding salaries for fifty new heads in customer service), or whether the policy change would only impact our financial accounting for expected future liabilities on the "balance sheet." Once we both agreed this was an accounting cost, and he realized that it was only the rules for using the time-off benefit that would change, he approved the proposed policy, and employees welcomed the improvement.

Why does this matter? Think about managing your business or company finances. You have sources of income that get deposited into your bank account. Those funds get disbursed day by day throughout the month for all kinds of expenses for inventory, payroll, utilities, credit card commissions, etc. And when the store manager wants something out of the ordinary (like an unbudgeted employee hire), and there is no precedent for this expense, you look at the cash flow position in your business account and make a decision. That is an example of "economic cost."

In a business context, there are multiple examples of accounting costs that do not impact cash flow. One is depreciation, referring to the decreasing value of assets over time. Another example is stock-based compensation which has no immediate economic cost but does have an accounting cost and has the potential for value dilution in the pockets of shareholders.

In summary, as the owner or leader of a company in business, whether you have one location or one thousand locations, it is critical that you understand the flow of money and embrace the consequences of financial decisions on your business. Now let's move on to identifying the people groups engaged in our case study and most prevalent in the eco-system of business. As we do, we'll uncover the challenges leaders face trying to get everyone to play well together.

SECTION TWO

Author's Objective: *Identify* the key stakeholder groups and what they value. Connect to the leader's struggle to satisfy the expectations of each group.

Chapter Three:

People Groups

See the money, wanna stay for your meal
Get another piece of pie, for your wife
Everybody wanna know, how it feel
Everybody wanna see, what it's like
Baby wanna be a queen, well alright
We all deserve the finer things, in this life.
("The Greenback Boogie")[1]

There are eight key populations of people within the eco-system of Ted Hanson's business. In this chapter, we will work our way top down in the order Ted (and eventually his team of leaders) encountered these people who would become stakeholders, and on whom he was highly dependent. When you begin a new business from scratch, you might think that attracting customers would come first, but that was not the case with Ted Hanson. In the beginning, he only had two things going for him: an idea worth pursuing, and a top-notch reputation in the community. So, the first thing he needed was partners in the business.

Partners: Ted was acquainted with an assistant professor in the business department at Northern Illinois University, located right there in DeKalb just a few blocks from the downtown core. These two developed a friendship and spent hours together talking about the prospective business, the opportunities and challenges, the need for capital to purchase inventory, how many employees he would hire, and what would be the best location. Above all, together they would write and rewrite a business plan until it was ready for launch.

The second key partnership Ted nurtured was with the landlord, an elder statesman in town who owned several commercial properties, with standing buildings that could be retrofitted to accommodate a retail store. Because of Ted's reputation as a local firefighter — a hard-working, honest man with integrity and grit, these prospective partners were eager to work with him and see Ted succeed. Other partners with professional skills in finance and banking, accounting, employment law, and marketing came along as inaugural investors, coaches, and advocates for his success.

The learning here about partners is that you need them, even if they do not necessarily need you. Think about it — why would reputable professionals and business owners in the community want to partner with an untested small business owner with no prior experience? Unless they have an explicit reason not to, I have found that potential partners are typically drawn to cheer for an underdog like Ted.

Unfortunately, I have also encountered and worked with some businesspeople who just aren't that pleasant to be around. Some have questionable history, some are egotistical, others are elitist, and more than a few are just plain improper and condescending. If those were Ted's character attributes, there would be no company for us to discuss. But in this case, Ted was a solid citizen with a business plan. Check. Ted had a landlord who negotiated a reasonable plan for tenant improvements. Check. Ted had existing relationships with one or two banks in town. Check. From the onset, Ted's success with his stakeholder partners is a credit to his sound character and reputation.

Suppliers: Next, Ted needed to fill his retail space with inventory. He knew he needed to start small, and he only had so much floor space, so his initial inventory was in hardware, paint, and lumber. Remember that he wanted to be able to respond to customers with the statement, "yes, we've got that" — this would have a lasting impact on how he thought about inventory. He asked his contractor buddies and do-it-yourself friends in DeKalb what brands of merchandise they liked for quality and price. Based on their recommendations, Ted contacted a few potential suppliers and met with their representatives. These people are also in business and looking to grow market share and work with retailers who will sell their products to the end-customer.

Ted decided to focus on the Craftsman brand for tools, Grainger for hardware and general supplies, Pittsburgh Paints, and Georgia Pacific for wood products (later, through a series of events including a family inheritance and several timely purchases of forested land in the western US, the company would supply its own wood products to the stores). Ted was not in the best bargaining position as a neophyte business owner, but after reviewing his business plan these supplier reps signed on to participate in whatever success Hanson's Home & Hardware would create.

Advised by other experienced counselors, Ted negotiated good-faith terms for payment of the inventory 30–60 days after it was delivered to the store. This gave him an opportunity to sell the merchandise before he had to pay the supplier and reduced the need for an outflow of cash (which in the early days was in short supply). However, as time went on and there was an increase in customer demand from new locations, Ted and his team had to make some difficult decisions about inventory.

One such example was the temptation to add an automotive section to the store. Personally, I recall buying my first used car as a college student, and money was tight. Washing my own car, changing the oil, and replacing spark plugs were routines I could do much cheaper than taking it to the local Chevy dealer. A lot of Ted's customers did the same, hence the idea of potential inventory expansion into automotive parts and supplies. It came down to a decision of suppliers, pricing, and record of on-time delivery. While some of the signals were pointing to expand into this new category, Ted could not find a supplier he was willing to work with and so he eventually nixed the idea. At this stage, Ted had enough good experiences with suppliers to know how important these people were to the success of his business, and he wasn't willing to risk partnering with a supplier he could not trust to give him favorable terms.

Ted came to realize the value of his suppliers in the early years of being in business. However, to the general public, it was decades later during the 2020 COVID pandemic that the concept of the "supply chain" came front and center. Interruptions due to community health lockdowns and closed factories, with millions of illness-afflicted people around the globe unable to work, made it nearly impossible to keep the flow of goods coming like we all had grown accustomed. Store shelves were half empty, mechanical parts were unavailable, and merchants were unable to supply and serve customers due to circumstances out of their control.

You may recall news in the year 2021 of a huge tanker ship that ran aground in the Suez Canal, which bridges the Mediterranean Sea to the Red Sea, effectively making it difficult for trade to flow freely between the east and west globally. Over a nine-day period, this unexpected blockade prevented over 200 similar container ships from passing through the canal, effectively freezing in place up to 400,000 containers of trade goods from delivery to their respective markets.[2] (A typical 40-foot container has a load capacity of 36 tons.) These incidents have reinforced our understanding of the fragile nature of suppliers, supply chain and the modes of transportation for distributing goods to a global marketplace.

I trust you are convinced of the need to pay close attention to, and invest in your suppliers.

Employees: Hanson's Home & Hardware hours of operation were Monday through Saturday, 8:00 a.m. to 5:00 p.m. Ted figured he needed one full-time stock clerk, one full-time cashier, one part-time cashier, one full-time sales assistant, and one part-time sales assistant. That meant he needed to hire five people, train them, and get the team ready for the store grand opening.

Years later, when they had grown to 390 stores, the HomeSource company employed over 32,000 people in local stores, regional offices, and the corporate headquarters. To support a workforce of this size, HomeSource had over 100 executives headquartered in a dedicated building in downtown DeKalb, looking after every area of the company. Reporting to these executives were managers and directors, analysts, buyers, and all manner of subject matter experts that numbered close to 900 employees. Store managers, assistant store managers, and managers-in-training numbered close to 1000. Then, of course, total headcount in the stores was approximately 30,000 hourly workers. Let's take a quick look at each of the primary employee groups and what makes them unique (we will look more closely at their expectations for the business in the next chapter).

Executives: Eventually, HomeSource had over 100 executives in vice president and C-suite roles. Some of these leaders were family members. Some were among the first generation of store employees who grew up in the company and were promoted time and again to greater scope of responsibility. It is likely others were recruited from general industry backgrounds, some in retail and others from companies where the challenges and opportunities were similar to HomeSource.

As I alluded to earlier, executives are a different breed. They are distinctive in their education, their work experiences, their sphere of influence and in their expectations of other people. When it comes to their education, executives will not only have graduated from four-year universities, but typically from post-graduate degree programs as well. If you locate your business in DeKalb, Illinois, it is probable you have your share of NIU grads, but also talent from the University of Illinois, Loyola University, the University of Wisconsin, the University of Chicago, and Northwestern University. (Men and women who attend scholastically elite schools are making significant financial and time investments in their education. They are commonly referred to as "blue chip graduates" due to the quality of their education and the probability of success in the marketplace.)

Executives are also distinctive in the expectations they have for themselves and for other employees on their teams. Most executives I have worked with thrive in a "performance environment," where each person is expected to give of themselves in a manner that exceeds expectations to a high degree. These expectations are almost always linked to the business plan for revenue growth, for profitability, for customer acquisition, for expense controls, and for product and service innovation. In my experience, executives tend to grade their own job performance favorably, and grade others less favorably. To state the obvious, executives are also rewards driven to the nth degree. A well-known axiom comes to mind: "what gets measured (and rewarded), gets done." The implied reversal is powerful: that a leader is prone to quickly lose focus on things that may be urgent or even important if there isn't a "carrot of reward" waiting at the finish line.

Considering their distinctive education and expectations, you may be surprised to know that many executives are quite disconnected from the general employee population. We will explore this further in a subsequent chapter.

Managers: This group of people organizationally resides between the front-line workers (doing the work of the business) and the executives who are accountable for the business outcomes. Managers are critically important to the success of the company. Once Hanson's Home & Hardware began to grow and open new locations, Ted could not be everywhere at once. He needed to nurture a core of managers who knew the business and could be trusted with assets such as inventory, customer interactions, payroll, and employee relations. In a word, managers are **responsible** for the day-to-day operation of all business activity.

Managers are typically people selected from the population of front-line workers who are better performers, more reliable, able to enthusiastically work with customers, demonstrate teamwork, and show some interest in growing their career with the company. The work of a manager is typically focused on supervising people, but not always. Managers can also be individual contributors whose role is to manage a process, a program, a project, a system, or initiative that upper management wants to promote.

One of my trusted friends shared that this description of a manager reminded him of the highest-ranking enlisted persons in the US military. Their command of technical features and requirements is impeccable, and yet they also know how to expertly break it down and get lower ranking personnel to follow them. It really is a solid picture of the combination of skills required of managers in the context of business too.

My first role in business was a combination of individual contribution and supervising one other person — a classic example of a new manager. The person I supervised was an experienced woman who knew what we needed to do, but she did not inspire the confidence of upper management.

It is not uncommon for people (like me) to be hired into or promoted to managerial positions with little to no experience of managing people, or competency in the role, and with very little training. They are expected to learn on the job and do it quickly. As such, they make an honest effort to do good work, but they also make a lot of mistakes. Here is a sampling of mine:

- *In an unsuccessful attempt at humor, I made poorly timed comments in front of another employee who was watching to see if I was a genuine person who could be trusted.*
- *Unintentionally, I released some very sensitive information to a group of general managers and did not proactively report the error to the CEO.*
- *To secure alignment with a trusted manager who reported to me, I raised my voice and displayed emotion that could only be described as "angry frustration."*
- *It became necessary to terminate the employment of a person on my team for good reasons, but I did so without the caring and kind demeanor that person deserved.*

I have just referenced four examples from the journal of missteps in my career and here is one interesting thing they all have in common: if I were to reach out to the people referenced above, and offer to check-in on how they are doing after all these years (this is something I do all the time, connecting with former colleagues), I do not expect any of them would return my call. Why? Because, on those days I did not behave professionally, I failed, and in so doing I was inappropriate, defensive, blaming, and insensitive. These are not the behaviors of people you want to see in the role of manager; and yet, this can be your reality in business. Managers may be untested, prematurely selected, marginally trained, and possibly good at doing the work but less competent at motivating and leading people who work on the front-line of your business.

Thankfully, that first assistant and I overcame the potential friction and worked well as a team, and to her credit she kept up her excellent contributions just like always. The team grew, and then after almost four years, I was promoted to a role at the corporate office. Like me, your company's managers aren't perfect, but these valued employees contribute to the success of the business at both the customer and corporate level.

Front-Line Workers: These are the remaining 30,000 employees at HomeSource. Most, if not all of us have experience in roles like these. My first real paying job was at the Rub-A-Dub Car Wash located on the corner of 82nd Avenue and Glisan Street in Portland, Oregon. My hourly wage was $1.00 per hour. I discovered a few things, like the pace was fast, managers yelled a lot, a person could get fired for messing up, and best of all you could make money if you worked hard. I liked making money, and I always have. Earlier in middle school I rode my bicycle delivering newspapers, and if the weather was poor, my kind mother would back the family car out of the garage and drive me around my delivery route. The last newspaper delivery stop was the donut shop, and the owner would pay me with two fresh-made maple bars every morning (that was cool!). In my senior year of high school, I stocked shelves at the national chain grocery store, and loaded purchases into customers' vehicles. My only complaint was with the grocery manager who refused to let me have a day off for some graduating-senior shenanigans. He knew I was a good kid and suggested it would be a better use of my time to show up for work on the day in question. I reluctantly agreed.

I have been a landscaper and a door-to-door salesman. I've worked the night shift for a janitorial service, loaded delivery trucks for a national transport company, manned the shipping desk for a parts supplier, sold men's furnishings in a department store, and coached a youth basketball team. Every one of these roles was operational, basic, functional, and with little to no authority. I was hired to do a job, show up on time, follow instructions, learn the work, make few mistakes, get along with teammates and be truthful with my timecard. In summary, this is a fairly accurate description of the working lives for millions of people in the United States.

Nationally, when looking at non-farm employment in the private sector, front-line workers (employed full-time) number close to 32 million people,[3] while part-time workers number 27 million people.[4] Let's call it an even 60 million people, working in various industries like healthcare, grocery/convenience/drug stores, retail, hospitality/restaurants, childcare/social services, construction and repair trades, trucking/warehousing, cleaning/janitorial services, manufacturing, and public transportation.

The jobs held by front-line workers in these industries typically have fewer requirements for education and experience than professional and managerial jobs. It follows that these jobs are almost always compensated at lower rates than other jobs in the company, which contributes to the concentration of wealth at the top of the educational/career pyramid. Additionally, the demography of people who occupy front-line jobs contributes to the gender pay gap. It is not my intent to debate the root causes of the gender pay gap here, but only to point out that a high representation of females in front-line jobs — when compared to representation in managerial and executive jobs — does impact the pay data. These are generalized descriptions of the front-line worker, and not meant to discredit the hundreds of thousands of females and/or immigrant business owners who overcame cultural obstacles and found success anyway, many of whom are my friends or people with whom my family does business.

We should acknowledge a sub-set of front-line workers who make the conscious choice to avoid the supervisory responsibilities so integral to being a manager. They like interacting directly with the customer or supplier. They like doing the work they are trained to do with singular focus, and without the distractions associated with job roles higher up on the organizational chart. They like being able to finish their scheduled shift, go home and not worry about the health of the enterprise or the demands of corporate bureaucracy. It is a tradeoff they are willing to make, even if wage growth is limited and the opportunity for promotion less likely.

The irony is that the work of 60 million front-line workers is core to the business of companies who employ them. (In a further irony, I do not know of a single company executive who was deemed to be an "essential worker" during the recent pandemic.) Front-line workers manage the business activity, moving products, selling merchandise, interacting with customers, caring for patients, administering processes and re-stocking inventory. Yet they hold very little influence or power over the direction of the business, nor do they have access to the information and reporting that managers do. However, what they do control is the quality of customer experience and the reputation of your business in the community. Don't you find it remarkable that the lowest-ranking employees in your company have the most direct and long-lasting influence on your customers and your brand? I do. Almost every company I know is organized this way, and per capita investments in the front-line worker are funded at levels significantly less than other stakeholder groups. More to come on that topic.

Customers: Every good business plan addresses the potential for attracting and retaining customers. Is there a current demand for your product or service, or is the business innovating into territory that is unknown? Is there a customer need? Will people go for it, and buy it at the price you set? Will the customer purchase from you again, creating a sustainable demand for whatever you are selling?

Ted Hanson had a few things going for him (in the language of business these are called "tailwinds"). First, there was an existing customer need for hardware, paint, and wood products. Second, he chose to invest in a market size (10,000–30,000 residents) that could support home improvement shopping without attracting large national chains. And third, he was a local guy who people knew and trusted.

Other aspects of his business venture created uncertainty and risk (these are called "headwinds"). Would customers embrace the one-stop-shop experience, or stick with the smaller stores in town? How much customer loyalty was out there for the taking? How much elasticity was in the market for his goods (this refers to customers spending money in good economic times and in bad times)? Would his suppliers come through as promised and would his employees treat customers well?

If you stop and think about it, you have experienced a wide range of customer interactions over the course of your life. Some are not acceptable, with you telling yourself, "Never again"; others are so-so, not horrible but not great; and a few are on your customer highlight reel, making you a repeat customer who refers that business to others as well.

In business today, companies work at getting their customers to rate the quality of the product and the efficiency of the service interaction. Typically, customer satisfaction (focused on specific interactions), customer loyalty (net promoter score), and ease of customer experience are tracked regularly and reported to senior executives. The foundation of these metrics is self-reported by customers, which makes you wonder whether the data is skewed based on the time and effort it takes for customers to participate. I should also mention that more companies today have an executive role whose primary focus is on the customer experience.

The most common customer tailwinds in business today are brand awareness, product quality, selection, availability, ease of access, and overall economic strength.

> *The Conference Board Consumer Confidence Survey® reflects prevailing business conditions and likely developments for the months ahead. This monthly report details consumer attitudes, buying intentions, vacation plans, and consumer expectations for inflation, stock prices, and interest rates.*[5]

The most common customer headwinds in business today are inflation/price, a plethora of competitors, poor customer interactions, brand reputation, industry regulation, and breaches in cyber security.

In summary, customers have high expectations. They do not like to be ignored, mistreated, or disappointed. They will be loyal to you, but only if you consistently deliver and are loyal to them. Repeat business must be earned, or they will shop your competitors and talk smack about you on social media. They know what they need, sort of. You see, many of the world's most sellable products did not exist a generation ago. The magic of innovation created new products with customers scrambling to get one at any cost. Think lottery tickets, enhanced water, gourmet coffee, cloud computing, smart phones, e-commerce, electric vehicles, and virtual reality. The stickiness of these innovations with customers gives immense hope to every entrepreneur and business owner who is wanting to light a fire under a new generation of customer demand and delight.

Investors: A profitable, successful business with hordes of satisfied and returning customers eventually attracts the outside world of investment. In the early days of Hanson's Home & Hardware, the only real investors were the Hanson family along with a few select individuals who either gifted or loaned seed money to help get the business started. While this type of funding was important and foundational, the greatest investment at the time was the sacrificial effort of the Hanson family themselves, sometimes referred to as "sweat equity."

As the business found opportunities to grow, Ted cautiously and methodically invited well-to-do people in the markets he served to provide working capital in exchange for a small percentage of the company. Decades into the life of the business, the private equity firms began to inquire about Hanson's interest in an entirely different relationship between owner and investors. PE firms are well-funded from the cash invested by their limited partners and the cash generated by the multiple companies they own. Their proposal to Hanson's Home & Hardware was an infusion of cash to the Hanson family and the initial investors (known as a "liquidity event") in exchange for outright ownership of the company. Later, after the PE firm bought all the Hanson shares, a broader contingent of investors was invited to experience ownership in the HomeSource company when it went public ten years later.

As you can probably figure out, not all investors are created equal. Some put in a little, some put in a lot. Some have influence or control over how the business is operated, most do not. Some are in it for the long-haul, others (like day-traders) are not. Some want the company to succeed, some do not (you can do your own research on the practice of investor "short selling").

Some care about your customers, and some care about a "cause agenda" more than anything.

Community: This population of people is not often mentioned in books about business. In our context, community refers to the people who directly interface with your company, those who reap tangible benefit from the location of your business activity, and others who would like to influence the decisions you make as an owner or leader. Fellow business owners in the community typically welcome the presence of other successful ventures (under the theory that a "rising tide lifts all boats"), if the competition is fair, and the economy grows. Civic officials usually fall all over themselves at the prospect of new and emerging business interests in the community. (In the later years of our life together, my wife and I gravitated to smaller cities and towns, where we see gleeful enthusiasm when a new business opens.) When a new business opens, employment grows, so does tax revenue and improvements to infrastructure get funded. Economic vitality with employment opportunity and new residents usually translates into good news for member-based organizations such as local churches, civic clubs, commercial networks, recreation venues and amateur sport leagues.

However, even as businesses grow, you need to be aware of a few unintended consequences that may impact the relationship with local communities. **First, not everyone in the community will embrace the change that comes from growth**. Experiencing change is not necessarily the first choice for some people. They may like things just the way they are, or they may not appreciate the influx of new people with modern ideas and apparent lack of appreciation for local customs. **Second, the presence of new business, growing employment and rising population may be viewed as a risk** to the well-intentioned members of the community accountable for basic services such as police and fire protection, schools, roads, highways and city parks. I have personally seen a circumstance where a housing developer requested city approval on a plan to build several hundred new residences, without any funding commitments to these important services in the community (the public was outraged, the city council balked, and the developer walked away from the project). And **third, the presence of new and thriving business ventures energizes the not-for-profit interests** in the local community who see your company as a funding source for their organization. While this expectation of charitable contribution may be reasonable, some local businesses are not fully prepared for the "popularity" that comes with their success. This begs the question of who has the power or right to lay claim to a company's resources. Varying schools of thought advocate for the investor, or the worker, or the regulator or even society at large. A business owner intent on building strong relationships with the community needs to have a well-thought-out, articulated point of view on this question that will be proactively shared with local leaders and any member of the community as appropriate.

Now that we have identified the eight key people groups that reside in the eco-system of business, wouldn't it be nice if everyone would simply cooperate and work together to make all businesses succeed? Unfortunately, in my experience, that can be difficult for the business owners and designated leaders to achieve. Why? Because each of these people groups has expectations, agendas and economic realities of their own that feed into the eco-system. You might say in effect, that you really have very little control over the existence of these people groups, and that (contrary to your wishes) they behave somewhat independently when it comes to the vision, values, and strategy of your company. Simply put, you should expect these stakeholders will act according to their own self-interest, and it is advisable that you accept that reality. What makes this even more daunting and awkward is that these stakeholder groups often have competing interests, even from within each other, and some may be totally disconnected from your primary objectives as the business leader.

I know this grates on you. You are accountable and responsible for what happens in your business — and your expectation is that everything is within your control. But in most situations, it just doesn't work that way. You are highly dependent on others, and this circumstance makes you uneasy. Let's see if we can take the tension you are feeling at this moment and move to something more constructive and hopeful.

Chapter Four:

Competing Interests

Work Wellness Institute[1]

Maybe this is the first time you have acknowledged how disconnected stakeholders can be from each other, and most specifically the misalignment between what they want and what you have been hired to deliver. Facing this uncomfortable reality, you have three choices:

1. Ignore it. Hope the voices are ineffective in their advocacy.
2. Fight it. Adopt an adversarial mindset and crush the opponent as often as possible.
3. Embrace it. Find perspective, look for positive intent and redirect the energy.

Let's assume you're ready to embrace it (option #3 above) and willing to work effectively with these key stakeholders.

Considering that, let's explore how each people group expresses themselves, and we will identify their primary interests.

Partners: In many ways, you will find this population is the smallest in number and largest in tolerance when it comes to the ups and downs you will likely experience in business. These people are your most loyal and hopeful cheerleaders. They want you to succeed, they support your business plan, they appreciate the positive impact you are having on the community of employees and customers. (If this description does not fit the partners in your company, it is possible you need different partners, or maybe a new business plan.)

Let's imagine that a wealthy supporter loaned Ted Hanson $50,000 in the year 1982 to help him get started, asking that his stake in the business be valued after ten years and liquidated. And suppose the gain replicated the S&P 500 index, and the original investment is worth a valuation of $280,000 after ten years.[2] That is great, but you might be surprised to know that while the financial gain was welcomed, the partner simply wanted to win. Partners like winning, and they each have their own internal standard of what winning means.

Here is a true story example. Two brothers immigrated to the US and built a software company they sold a few years later for $22 million. They used these funds to stake a California winery which proved to be very successful, and 15 years later sold the winery to an Australian company for $1 billion.[3] It is a scenario like this (not often repeated, but it does happen) that drives partners with access to capital to team up with business owners whom they trust and build on innovative ideas that generate huge wins.

You have probably watched on television more than one broadcast of the National Football League. It is common for the camera to occasionally focus on the "owner's box" where a group of well-dressed men and women, many of whom you do not recognize, are expressing emotions that make it clear whether their team is winning. One of the most well-known figures is Dallas Cowboys owner Jerry Jones, who is quite expressive. In the moment he is featured on camera, you are not left wondering whether his team is winning or losing. But regardless of the outcome of any specific play-call, or whether his team leads or trails at halftime, the only emotion that really matters is the one you see once the final clock is at 0:00. Partners like to win, and whether it's by 3 points or 30 points they will express jubilation. **Winning** is the thing that matters.

Suppliers: This people group helps you get started in business, they serve as the backbone of your supply chain of goods and services, they are the conduit between you and the manufacturer, and you hope they evolve and grow as your business grows and diversifies. In the Hanson Home & Hardware story, you may have wondered what factors influenced Ted's preference for the suppliers he chose.

You may not know that in the 1980s, The Sears Roebuck Company was the largest and most successful department store in the US and owned the very reputable Craftsman brand of tools. W.W. Grainger had a geographical connection, founded and headquartered in northern Illinois. Pittsburgh Paints wanted to increase their market share in the Midwest at the time, and in their zeal to expand they offered Ted a very attractive discount program. And Georgia Pacific owned forested land adjacent to property in the Pacific Northwest owned by the Hansons' extended family.

Unlike the partner, the supplier is in a business of his own with an income statement and expectations regarding revenue and profit. The supplier buys from manufacturers (his supplier) and sells to you (his customer). Therefore, the supplier has a financial incentive to buy low and sell high, whereas you also have the identical incentive to buy low (from suppliers) and sell high (to customers). I hope you see the potential friction that can often occur in this relationship.

You may recall we covered "gross margin" in Chapter Two, which is the difference between the cost of purchasing goods and the revenue from selling those goods. This difference is also commonly known as the "mark-up," and is what enables a company to be in business. The gross margin is top of mind for the manufacturer, for the supplier, and for your company because that is how everyone makes money and stays in business. Here is an example of the cost structure on a gallon of paint that Ted sold in his store:

	$$	%
Direct Manufacturer Cost	$ 2.35	
Manufacturer Mark-up	$ 7.05	300%
Supplier Cost	$ 9.40	
Supplier Mark-up	$ 4.70	50%
Retailer Cost	$ 14.10	
Retailer Mark-up	$ 14.10	100%
Customer Price	$ 28.20	

In some cases, the business works directly with a distributor of many products from multiple manufacturers. All three entities in this chain of transactions are in business to pay their expenses and come out with a profit in the end. So, to survive, they need to set the price for the goods or services within reason for the product and industry, pay their employees, and show a return to themselves and their investors. As the face to the customer, you can only push your supplier so far based on the economics of his business.

Going back to the football analogy, you will often hear coaches tell players (and the media) that the goal is to compete. Do your best, leave it all out there on the field, give maximum effort, and let the other team know you are there to force the outcome. A coach might say, "if the other team prevails, let's at least make them earn it." With suppliers, they are in the middle between you and the manufacturer with all parties interconnected and needing to stay in business. This is exactly the time and place for win-win negotiating principles, where there is a give-and-take in items of value that benefits both parties. For suppliers, they do not want to obliterate the other guy, **competing** is what matters.

Executives: I am tempted to use the word "leader" instead of "executive." However, I learned a valuable lesson about leadership during my years at Amazon. As the company grew, we partnered with the CEO to define a set of leadership principles. These principles applied to every employee in the company who held a salaried position. Everybody, whether your title indicated leadership or not. It didn't matter if you managed people or not. It didn't matter if this was your first professional job out of college. Everyone was expected to display leadership principles. Executives are given huge opportunities to be leaders, but not all leaders are executives.

That said, who are executives and what do they value? Previously, I talked about their distinctiveness so now let's dig a little deeper into their motivations. The people who are appointed to these roles are held accountable and responsible for the general health of the company. They represent the major and minor lines of business. They possess specialty skills in the areas of finance, marketing, human resources, and law. How well this level of talent performs can make or break your company.

In the last chapter, I observed that in my experience some executives can become disconnected from the general population of employees. They typically only hold meetings with you if your title warrants it and are unlikely to ask for your opinion.

They do not spend time sharing a meal with regular employees (I once interviewed for a leadership role with a global consumer brand where executives had their own private dining room), and most likely you will hardly ever see them in your department or schedule a visit to your store. Some of this is a function of size and the distribution of company locations all over the map. But in truth, these executive behaviors are usually a matter of either personal choice (due to introversion or insecurity) or professional choice (competing demands from priorities, time-sensitive deliverables or maintaining focus).

The good news is there are exceptions. Many CEOs see themselves as guardians of culture and ambassadors of goodwill. They welcome opportunities to be messengers of information to stakeholders. One example is Jeff Bezos, founder and CEO at Amazon who was often seen in the cafeteria at a table with employees just talking and laughing over lunch. He was the voice employees wanted to hear at every internal town hall meeting; he was the voice every analyst and investor wanted to hear on the quarterly earnings call; and I do not recall him missing a single such gathering over seven years.

The president of Walgreens USA had a routine of inviting other leaders to join him for store location visits to meet customers, solicit feedback from employees, and treat managers and pharmacists to dinner. The Chief People Officer at Microsoft invited an entire division to enjoy a private museum party complete with live music and a food extravaganza, giving all of us an opportunity to be ourselves and grow our capacity for fun and teamwork.

According to a study by the Deloitte Consulting Group, 91% of executives agree with the statement that "leaders in our company care for the welfare of employees." Alarmingly, the Deloitte study also discovered that only 56% of employees think that their company's executives care about them (Deloitte, 2022).[4] That is quite a disconnect.

So, what do executives care about? Or asked differently, what motivates and drives executives to behave, prioritize, and make decisions like they do? In my experience, it is ambition, achievement and acquisitiveness. Maybe I am scarred by dozens of conversations with executives making $5 million plus per year, who threaten to quit if they don't get more.

"The most common reaction of the human mind to achievement is not satisfaction but craving for more ... always on the lookout for something better, bigger, tastier." (Yuval Noah Harari)[5]

And yet this executive drive shows up in a lot of constructive and defensible ways, like building a business, attracting great talent, meeting with key customers, growing market share, and keeping up appearances with investors. Some executives are self-described builders, they love innovation and finding new ways of meeting customer needs. In the process, they advocate for larger teams, work to secure funding for new product research, and acquire nascent companies to harvest and redeploy valuable assets. In some cases, they may be out of their depth, so they retain external advisers and coaches to help them increase their awareness, judgement, and executive skill.

One executive who is not out of his depth is the renowned sports agent, Scott Boras. This guy is well-educated, incredibly smart, successful, and the subject of much attention in the world of major league baseball. Scott Boras has created an ingenious business model that is built around the principle of self-aggrandizement and the promise of record-setting wealth for his clients (and himself). The premise is quite simple: attract professional baseball player clients with a history of success and eligible for free-agency; use analytics, forecasting, and marketing to predict even greater success for that player/client; and sell the multi-year, record-setting, fully guaranteed pay package to billionaire owners who desperately want to win at any cost and have nothing to lose. What Boras doesn't publicize is that many of his clients will not deliver a world championship to their respective teams. He also doesn't want you know that many teams' general managers and owners refuse to do business with him, maybe because they remember his association with "the worst contract in the history of sports."[6] The contract was for a baseball pitcher named Stephen Strasburg whom Boras signed to the Washington Nationals team for seven years and $245 million. Under this new contract, Mr Strasburg pitched a total of 30 innings and retired from the game.[7] No apologies, no regrets, no refunds. Many people believe such greed-based deals are ruining baseball, with one writer stating, "Now that Boras is around, all honor and loyalty is dead."[8]

You may have had different experiences, but many of the executives I know have strong appetites for more revenue, more profit, more autonomy, more credibility, more recognition, and more executive pay. There are many powerful forces in play that contribute to oversized increases in executive pay,[9] however the corporate data trend seems clear:

> *From 1978 to 2021, CEO pay based on realized compensation grew by 1,460%, far outstripping S&P stock market growth (1,063%) and top 0.1% earnings growth (which was 385% between 1978 and 2020). In contrast, compensation of the typical worker grew by just 18.1% from 1978 to 2021.* (Economic Policy Institute, 2022)[10]

Incredibly, some wealthy executives are even seeking to defy the mortality tables by funding research on longevity and immortality, presuming greater life expectancy will allow them to solve the mega-issues plaguing the planet (excuse my sarcasm).[11] While these pursuits could be rationalized as good for society, some executives will do **anything** for more, including breaking the law. Enron CEO, Jeffrey Skilling, is a convicted felon who defrauded investors and was sentenced to 25 years in prison.[12] Wealth manager, Bernie Madoff, broke the law; his clients lost billions and he died in prison.[13] Elizabeth Holmes, former CEO at Theranos, was convicted of fraud for lying to partners, customers, and investors.[14] Nikola Motor founder and former CEO, Trevor Milton, portrayed himself as an innovative disruptor of the transportation industry but was convicted of investor fraud and nearly tanked his company.[15] Crypto genius Sam Bankman-Fried, in another fraud case, was recently sentenced to 25 years in prison.[16] These executives took "more" to the extreme.

I know from personal experience that not all executives are greedy and self-absorbed. Some in the ultra-wealthy class have exhibited their philanthropic bent by signing the Giving Pledge.[17] Billionaire Warren Buffet is well-known for living in the same modest home he purchased decades ago, driving a well-used sedan and donating much of his wealth to philanthropic causes. But in the spirit of understanding the general motivations and agendas of executives as a stakeholder group, we can state that **accumulation** is what matters.

Managers: In a typical company, there are 20 managers for every one executive. Managers carry all kinds of generic titles — including director, manager, supervisor, and principal — while others have job-specific manager titles such as attorney, controller, business partner, or leader. The original intent of the manager category was to denote a person who manages other people, who has direct reports and supervises the quality of their work. In the modern workforce, managers also have work of their own (apart from their direct reports). In some cases, such as with project and program managers, managers will work collaboratively across multiple teams without having subordinates report directly to them.

The role of manager is seen as the next step above front-line worker and includes a new set of responsibilities the person has not experienced before. These are likely to include people supervision, performance management, budgeting, scheduling, ordering, inventory control, interface with suppliers, and adherence to product and policy standards. Since the company is highly invested in the success of these managers, who have daily responsibility for running the business, many companies intentionally create training departments, curricula, and certifications that acknowledge the importance of managerial roles across all divisions, disciplines, and geographies.

People who sign up for manager jobs typically have ambitions to increase their pay, influence, visibility, and value to the business. When interviewing for manager jobs, the candidate will normally inquire about training, promotional opportunities, size of organization, and how to get ready for the next step in their career. We could dig deeper into the psyche of people who function as managers but suffice it to say that **advancement** certainly matters.

Front-Line Workers: No group of people in the eco-system of business is more diverse than the front-line worker — and no more essential. The term "essential worker" became acutely important during the COVID pandemic of 2020–2022, as government authorities classified certain types of work that had to get done — no matter what. These types of essential work included access to food and fuel, healthcare, financial services, the routines of uninterrupted interstate transport, and a few others.

In a non-pandemic world, just try to imagine how the quick-service food industry would instantly collapse without front-line workers. Or the multi-billion-dollar grocery industry. Or the hospitality industry. Or the vast industry of construction trades such as electrical, plumbing, roofing, and masonry.

One of the best ways to make the point is to imagine what our economy would look like at the extremes. Imagine owning a business, or being a customer of a business, where front-line workers did not exist. The result is utter chaos, collapse, disappointment, and the highest form of failure. Now imagine what it would be like if 100% of the available jobs in this country could be described as front-line work. There would be less need for higher education; fewer people skilled at programming, planning, or marketing; and practically no one experienced in managing and leading a large enterprise. Do you see the point? We need front-line workers, but they are not skilled nor capable of doing everything that is required to run a successful business.

Whereas executives are driven to accumulate, and managers are driven to seek advancement, I find that front-line workers have a more basic drive — they simply want to make it from one paycheck to the next. Front-line workers tend to have more job satisfaction, better work-life balance, and stronger interface with customers than do their colleagues in the managerial and executive ranks. However, these benefits come at a cost; it's the cost of basic-only education, lower wages, little influence, and infrequent opportunity for advancement. As we stated in Chapter Three, this may be a bargain that front-line workers are willing to make in exchange for not having to worry or care about work during their off-work hours. However, there is usually an economic consequence to this choice. So, like most other front-line workers, they settle into a routine and focus on what really matters to them, **getting by**.

Customers: Consider the improbability of having a great business model, but without any customers. So, what would be the point? There is no question that the presence or absence of customers has tremendous influence over the success and failure of a business. You can build it, but if they don't come you will not survive. "The failure rates of businesses show that around

20% fail in their first year and only about half of businesses are still standing after 5 years."[18]

The first-year failure rate suggests that customers did not show up in numbers large enough to get the business off the ground. The five-year failure rate suggests that customers may have been initially attracted to purchase goods and services from this business, but that the quality of interaction and meeting of expectations was so poor that customers took their business elsewhere.

Thousands of studies, articles, and books have been published on the expectations and purchasing habits of customers. Let's look at this complex subject more simply by suggesting just a few basics.

- Customers have a real or perceived need.
- Customers prefer to have purchase options.
- Customers have funds to complete a purchase transaction.
- Customers look for the highest quality at the lowest price.
- Customers have expectations for when their purchase will arrive, and how well the purchased item meets their needs.
- Customers believe that repeat business must be earned.

Do you recall from an earlier chapter how Ted Hanson had a vision for how to respond to all customer requests? Is there better music to the ears of a customer inquiry than the words, "Yes, we've got that"? You see, Ted knew the power of fine-tuning his inventory based on what he learned listening to customers. He also knew what the other stores in town did and did not carry on their shelves. He understood that customers have choices, and he wanted his customers to choose Hanson's Home & Hardware time and time again.

What I haven't told you about the Hanson story is that as the economy grew and the home improvement industry burgeoned at the seams, new competition came to town. In some cases, it was a direct regional or national competitor, and in other cases the big box retailers showed up with huge warehouse-sized stores featuring thousands of items in their inventory. But Ted had the reputation, the goods, the relationships, and the customer service — a full solution that his competitors could only hope for.

In the early days of Amazon, they summarized customer expectations with three simple words: selection, price, and convenience. The focus on <u>selection</u> led Amazon to expand inventory beyond books alone to fill up their "virtual shelves" with just about anything a customer would need (Amazon announced in 2023 that customers will be able to purchase new vehicles at Amazon.com).[19] The focus on <u>price</u> led potential customers to "warehouse deals," replenishment discounts, Prime days, and Black Friday/Cyber Monday holiday bargains. The focus on <u>convenience</u> led to third-party sellers, free shipping, same day delivery, Prime membership, and a seamless online shopping experience. At the end of the day, what matters most to customers is **finding value**.

Investors: Next, we come to the people group that publishes a scorecard of how you are doing as a business. If you are a publicly traded company, this scorecard gets refreshed and published every non-holiday business day, on 252 occasions in a typical calendar year.

These stakeholders have assets they are looking to invest and the capital markets have a decades-long track record of paying out average annual returns of 8%. In real terms, this means that a $100,000 investment is on average likely to grow into a $200,000 asset in approximately ten years. Unless an investor is wildly speculative, such a return is for most people quite acceptable over the long term.

So, what criteria does an investor use to decide in which companies to invest? Here is a real-life example from 1996 when the government eased regulations which enabled cable companies like @Home Network, a high-speed internet cable provider, to offer internet telephony to its customers. In 1999, @Home purchased the internet portal Excite in a merger valued at $6.7 billion.[20] This was, at the time, the largest merger of two internet companies and it looked like a sure-fire investment opportunity.

Let's suppose you had $3000 to invest. And then imagine what would have to happen for a $3000 investment to turn into something worth only $28.

> *The merger between Excite and @Home fell disastrously short of expectations. The new Chief Executive worked from his home in Massachusetts and the Chief Financial Officer lived in LA, flying in only once per week to the Bay Area to conduct business. Both executives were part of the former Excite executive team. More significantly, expenses ran far ahead of revenues. The burst of the dot-com bubble in March 2000 and the subsequent collapse of the Internet advertising market further limited the company's prospects by making it harder to raise investor money to keep the company afloat in the absence of retained earnings. By 2001, the company was running out of cash. The stock which once soared at $128.34 a share in the first quarter of 1999 and had a market cap of $35 billion had fallen to $1 a share by the third quarter of 2001 when the company formally filed for Chapter 11 bankruptcy protection.*[21]

During this same era, I recall investing in thriving telecom companies like MCI, WorldCom, and Lucent Technologies. After years of delayed consumer adoption, regulatory difficulty, mismanagement, leadership transitions, and market dynamics no one predicted, I sold my shares in all these companies at pennies on the dollar. Such investments can be fickle, and always carry some element of risk as well as the promise of return. The best investors throw as much analysis and quantitative research as possible at the opportunity. They look at history; they look at leadership; they look at financials; they look at the business plan; they look at the market demand for the products and services. They look at everything they can legally get their hands on, and then make decisions on where to invest, for how much, and for how long.

And once they invest in your company, they own you. In aggregate, the investors outside the walls of your firm are likely to own as much as 100% of your company. Harvard Business Review reported in 2022 that "institutional investors (which may offer both active and passive investment funds) own 80% of all stock in the S&P 500."[22] And that doesn't count the individual investors who own fractionally small pieces of your company.

So, you tell me, is this a population you need to know, understand, and dedicate your time and attention to? You are smart, you think I have made the case, and you answer in the affirmative. However, more than a few CEOs delegate this important relationship-building activity to the investor relations team. Sure, the CEO meets with the Board of Directors occasionally, who are elected by shareholders to represent their interest; convenes a meeting annually with Wall Street analysts who follow their company and make recommendations to shareholders; and shakes hands with any investors who may attend the company annual meeting.

I have been one or two doors away from top executives for parts of four decades, and I have had a view of how they spend their time. Outside of these modest connections I just described, only occasionally have I witnessed a leadership team strategically initiate and activate long-term relationships with investors. For a people group with such deep influence and interest in your company, it's incredible how little attention they receive from top company executives. That said, while I do think a strong relationship matters (more on that later), that's not what motivates this people group. What matters most to investors is a **return** on their investment.

Community: Picking up on the few thoughts we have already shared about "community," it may be true that not everyone in the community is happy to see your business or company in town. But rather than focus on the negative, which may or may not be your reality, let's look at the segment of your community who celebrates your business, wants you to stay, hopes that you will thrive and expects that you will share the fruit of your success among a variety of interests in the community. In the end, your community wants to retain the best of what it offers, adopt new practices that strengthen a sense of belonging and tap into sources of funding that can improve quality of life for all residents.

Commerce is the lifeblood of a community. The basic elements of our capitalist foundations are all in play around the commercial activity generated within your community. Have you ever had the experience of passing through a very small community out in the middle of nowhere? Where there is no gas station, no post office, no grocery store and no place to eat a hot meal, there is usually nothing but a home or two scattered about with no neighborhoods and no thriving community. You see, business activity and the community are inseparable, and inevitably the local and regional community is a large part of your company getting into and staying in business. You need them to survive, and they need you and all the products and services you offer, because in partnership with you the community gets to survive and sustain its quality of life. What matters most to the community is **preservation**.

There you have it, eight distinct stakeholder groups critical to the success of your business enterprise, each representing a motivation and drive that is unique to them:

- Partners: Winning
- Suppliers: Competing
- Executives: Accumulating
- Managers: Advancing
- Front-Line Workers: Getting By
- Customers: Finding Value
- Investors: Return
- Community: Preservation

Before we leave this discussion, let's consider one more population with **overlapping expectations**. These are the people who belong to more than one stakeholder group, like the partner who is also your customer, the front-line worker who is also your investor or the mayor's daughter who is also your employee. Your job as the executive and/or company leader is to find some sense of harmony that brings all these populations together, with a focus on some common mission or objective. The **bad news** is that these people groups have only a few things in common. The **better news** is that they all share at least one thing in common, and it's something you all can enthusiastically endorse (in principle). Unless the enterprise can succeed on this shared mission, no one will find much satisfaction.

Chapter Five:

Survive and Thrive

I think many people assume, wrongly, that a company exists simply to make money. Whilst this is an important result of a company's existence, we have to go deeper and find the real reasons for our being. As we investigate this, we inevitably come to the conclusion that a group of people get together and exist as an institution that we call a company so they are able to accomplish something collectively which they could not accomplish separately. They are able to do something worthwhile — they make a contribution to society. You can look around and still see people who are interested in money and nothing else, but the underlying drives come largely from a desire to do something else — to make a product — to give a service — generally to do something which is of value.
(David Packard)[1]

So, what is the shared expectation most people in the stakeholder groups can agree on? They have a vested interest in making sure the company will **survive and thrive**. When you create a scenario where your company continues to survive, whatever headwinds come your way, either self-inflicted or out of your control, you get to stay in business. Does that seem like a small concession to you? If it does, you should consider these examples:

1. **Blockbuster**: an American video rental store chain founded in 1985 reached its peak in 2004 with 9100 stores and 84,000 employees. Six years later, the company

declared bankruptcy and today operates a single store in Oregon that sells memorabilia.[2]
2. **Borders Group**: an American multinational book and music retailer founded in 1971 reached its peak in 2010 with almost 20,000 employees in over 500 Borders and Waldenbooks stores. Two years later the company filed for bankruptcy, liquidated its stores and sold its remaining assets to a competitor.[3]
3. **Compaq**: founded in 1982, Compaq was notably the first company to legally reverse engineer the IBM personal computer and rose to industry fame in the 1990s, becoming the largest supplier of desktop computers. Struggling to compete with computing giants HP and Dell, the company was acquired by HP in 2002 and the brand was used by HP for lower-end systems until being discontinued in 2013.[4]
4. **Polaroid**: an American company originally founded in 1937 and best known for its instant film and cameras, the company employed 21,000 people with $3 billion in revenue at its peak. The rise of new digital technologies led to a decline that caused the company to file for bankruptcy in 2001. Polaroid-branded consumer electronic products have been developed and released by various licensees globally.[5]
5. **Netscape**: best known for its internet browser and founded in 1994 by Jim Clark and Marc Andreessen, Netscape had a 90% market share but would later lose out to Microsoft's Internet Explorer.[6] By 2006, Netscape had just 1% of the market, was acquired by AOL, and was discontinued as a browser in 2008.[7]

You see, survival is not a sure thing. Former CEO of Intel, Andy Grove, once said, "success breeds complacency and complacency breeds failure."[8] If you do fail, everyone loses. But if you succeed at surviving, everybody has an opportunity to win. Survival is good for the stakeholders, and oddly enough, effective management of stakeholder interests is the path to survival.

Taking this one step further, unless leaders are facing dire circumstances that threaten their existence, I do not know too many leaders who simply want to survive — they want to **thrive**. Leaders know all too well that few experiences in business are better than growth in revenue, creating new products and finding new customers. However, dominance at the top of the pyramid is difficult to sustain.

Looking at the ten most highly valued companies in the world (the companies are ranked by market valuation, not annual revenues), we find that in the year 2000 the valuations were dominated by technology (Microsoft, Cisco, Intel and Nokia), consumerism (General Electric, Walmart, NTT Docomo) and energy (Exxon Mobil, Royal Dutch Shell).[9]

TOP COMPANIES OF 2000		
NAME	INDUSTRY	VALUE
MICROSOFT	Technology	$ 586 B
GENERAL ELECTRIC	Diversified	$ 477 B
CISCO	Technology	$ 366 B
WALMART	Retail	$ 260 B
EXXON MOBIL	Oil & Gas	$ 260 B
INTEL	Technology	$ 251 B
NTT DOCOMO	Telecommunications	$ 246 B
ROYAL DUTCH SHELL	Oil & Gas	$ 203 B
PFIZER	Pharmaceuticals	$ 202 B
NOKIA	Technology	$ 186 B

By comparison in the year 2023, we find the list is led by Apple, Microsoft, Saudi Aramco, Alphabet, and Amazon. In the current big-tech era, Nokia has lost almost 90% of its value, General Electric routinely under-performed for many years and then spun-off business units, while NTT Docomo has seen steady rates of customer defections to competing carriers. Now, technology companies account for 70% of the top ten.[9]

TOP COMPANIES OF 2023		
NAME	INDUSTRY	VALUE
APPLE	Technology	$ 3,030 B
MICROSOFT	Technology	$ 2,510 B
SAUDI ARAMCO	Oil & Gas	$ 2,080 B
ALPHABET	Technology	$ 1,520 B
AMAZON	Technology/Retail	$ 1,340 B
NVIDIA	Technology	$ 1,050 B
TESLA	Automotive	$ 887 B
BERKSHIRE HATHAWAY	Diversified	$ 753 B
META	Technology	$ 733 B
TAIWAN SEMICONDUCTOR MANUFACTURING	Technology	$ 535 B

In a state of being where your business and company is not only surviving but thriving, the partners win; the suppliers compete; the executives get paid; the managers get promoted; the front-line workers keep their jobs; the customers enjoy your products; the investors "push more chips onto the table," and the community welcomes your contributions to quality of life. We should note, however, that not every member of these people groups has a common understanding of how the rewards of a thriving business should be distributed. So, let's examine a few "thrive" scenarios and see who typically reaps the benefit.

It is not uncommon for a company to reduce its cash reserves by a **board-authorized repurchase of its own stock**. While this action is a benefit to stockholders and executives, reducing the number of shares on the open market and thereby increasing the value of their holdings, this action does little to benefit anyone else in the system. In fact, in my experience stock re-purchases may also be accompanied by downsizing and employment layoffs.

When companies perform well, you would think that **employee wages would increase**. However, the data indicates a very different reality. Think back to what we discussed earlier: CEO pay grew by 1460% while front-line employee pay grew by 18.1% over the same period. A reasonable interpretation is that employees were given wage increases that barely kept pace with inflation, while executives and investors continued to accumulate wealth at a record-setting pace — monopolizing their grip on the riches generated from a thriving business. In the face of all that however, the influences of labor market dynamics and voices of various cause activists continue to call for higher wages and benefits that seek to bring respect and dignity to the work of front-line employees.

If you are charging customers $1200 for a new iPhone 15 Pro Max, then why not **build yourself a new headquarters**, which Apple completed in 2017. "Apple Park, the company's second campus, is a massive ring-shaped building that took four years to build and cost over $5 billion (the land cost was estimated at US$160 million). It was first proposed by the late CEO, Steve Jobs, in 2006 and it is one of the most expensive buildings in the world."[10]

Or how about the new Sofi Stadium, the first indoor-outdoor sports and entertainment destination stadium built for $5 billion in Inglewood, CA by National Football League owner, Ted Kroenke.

> *Not only is this the home of the Los Angeles Chargers and the Los Angeles Rams, but the state-of-the-art stadium re-imagines the fan experience and will host a variety of events including Super Bowl LVI, the College Football Championship Game,*

and the Opening and Closing Ceremonies of the Olympic Games in 2028. Located on the site of a former racetrack, the stadium is the centerpiece of a 298-acre mixed-use development featuring retail, commercial offices, a hotel, residential units, and outdoor park spaces.[11]

Another frequent use of company reserves is to **invest in capital assets**. These could include construction of a new production facility, updating equipment used in the manufacturing process, refreshing IT capability, strengthening the security of customer accounts, purchasing real estate in new markets, paying down debt and many more. It could be easily argued that these types of investments are in the best interest of all stakeholder people groups, benefit the long-term health of the company, and support its growth strategy; but in reality, they may do very little in the short-term to benefit employees and customers.

Less frequent, but certainly impactful are significant **investments in employee benefits, employee well-being, and amenities that strengthen worker engagement and loyalty**. Never was this more apparent than during the COVID pandemic when employers created work-from-home options, subsidized the cost of home daycare, reimbursed employees for internet service fees, and much more. Many companies also voluntarily adopted wage increases, especially for front-line workers in the grocery and healthcare sectors of the economy. While the federal minimum wage remained at $7.25 per hour, employers such as Amazon, Target, Aetna, Bank of America, and Costco Wholesale (just to name a few) raised their starting hourly rate to two-to-three times the federal minimum. Concerned about the mental health of workers confined to home during the pandemic, many employers got creative, offering emotional/psychological support and services — absent the social stigma normally associated with such conditions. Investments of this type are squarely focused on the employee population, with many partners and investors expressing vocal support of these actions. Apparently, it is good business to demonstrate care and concern for the workforce, however many of these investments were paused or defunded post-pandemic.

Moving on, we note that according to Investor's Business Daily, about 400 companies in the S&P 500 **pay dividends to shareholders of record**, at an average yield of 2.64%. And 20% of these dividend-sharing companies yield as much or more than the 10-year Treasury.[12] If you are thinking that many investors get paid dividends on top of the increase in valuation of their shares, you are generally correct (there have been exceptions to the rule). Unless you are a public shareholder, or an employee who owns shares in the company, this use of cash reserves does little to satisfy the needs of other stakeholders in the eco-system.

A thriving business usually attracts the attention of people in your community, with the expectation that you fulfill your duty as a **good corporate citizen**. Many communities plan celebrations and festivals throughout the year, creating a shared experience that promotes fun and a sense of belonging. Larger communities are likely to feature museums (linked to local lore), historical places of interest (often noted in national registries), venues with naming rights and recreational groups for children and adults. These community endeavors may be partially funded by user fees and public tax dollars, but in my experience much of the funding for these community activities comes from private donors and business owners. Whether you are aware or not, members of your community notice when you participate in funding the annual Independence Day parade and fireworks display. They look for the name of your business in the local newspaper during graduation season to see if you fund academic scholarships. The presence of your business name on the outfield wall at Little League Stadium looks good to those who expect you to share your success with the community of customers that keeps you in business. Even better is your company name associated with the new urgent care health clinic in town, or the covered picnic facility in the central commons park. This often unstated "quid pro quo" is very real — the small and large business owner alike should be mindful and intentional of how it gives back to needs in the community. This is a critical investment that proves you belong.

One final possible use of cash reserves is to **acquire other companies**, with the objective of stimulating growth in terms of financials, customers, markets, products, and highly coveted technical and subject matter expertise. I was fortunate to play project team roles, and in some cases a leadership role in a few notable acquisitions during my career. These included a contract manufacturer in Malaysia (Tektronix), a software firm in Denmark (Navision), an e-commerce shoe retailer in Las Vegas (Zappos), an e-commerce consumer goods brand in New Jersey (Quidsi), an online pharmacy in Seattle (Drugstore.com) and a major retailer in the UK with multi-continent wholesale distribution (Alliance Boots). In every one of these circumstances, the acquiring company had a strategic purpose that was supported by leadership, the board of directors, investors, lending partners and regulators (when applicable). Sometimes the intent was focused on products, in other cases it was geographic reach, and in others it was about the skills and capabilities of the workforce. Regardless, there was momentum to expect that this utilization of cash reserves would benefit the growing enterprise.

CVS Health is an interesting study in this regard. Founded in the 1960s with humble beginnings in Rhode Island, CVS (previously known as the Melville Corporation) grew by acquiring rival regional drug store chains including Long's, Eckard's, and People's Drugs as well as pharmacy customers from grocers like Albertsons and Target. With strategic intent to broaden the focus on healthcare (and changing the company name to CVS Health), the period from 2006–2017 saw unprecedented growth with the acquisitions of Minute Clinics (in-store acute care), Caremark (a pharmacy benefit manager serving employer group health plans), Omnicare (long-term health services) and finally Aetna (consumer directed health insurance). From public information available on these transactions, it appears that CVS Health invested close to $100 billion to acquire these competitors and other adjacent businesses that supported their growth strategy.[13]

As of this writing, CVS is the clear winner in the pharmacy-healthcare industry over the past 20 years. They have redefined their mission and vision as a "healthcare company," they have diversified their portfolio of businesses with an omni-channel approach, they have outperformed the S&P 500, and they have generated an eight-fold return for their shareholders. They serve over 100 million customers each year, with about 50% of the customer contact in a variety of digital formats. Annual revenue now exceeds $200 billion and employment is at an all-time high (over 300,000).[14] Even when they occasionally reduce the labor force to achieve a more competitive cost structure, they do so by eliminating jobs that are not customer-facing.[15] However, not everything is perfect at CVS. Their store formats are inferior to Walgreens, they still lack a branded presence in some geographies, and they have a troubled partnership with the United Commercial & Food Workers Union which represents a segment of their employees.

Survive and thrive is a reality that most (if not all) of your stakeholder groups can support, although we have demonstrated that there is disagreement on how to reinvest the cash reserves generated by a growing and successful business. We have just touched on a few of the most common approaches companies take, and in summary we can state that none of these will be satisfactory to everyone. Even a thriving business struggles with the collision of competing interests and needs strong leadership to maintain the equilibrium required for enterprise health.

Chapter Six:

Intersection Chaos

> *I won't need to define organizational chaos. You know exactly what I am talking about: shifting priorities, unclear direction, unstable processes, unhappy customers, disengaged employees … I'm talking about the undesirable type of chaos — self-inflicted chaos — the disorder and confusion that your organization creates on its own and, by extension, has the power to reduce or eliminate completely. Left unchecked, chaos destroys everything that's good about an organization, its products, and the people who make them. Chaos is the enemy of any organization that strives to be outstanding. (Karen Martin)*[1]

I love metaphors. People who know me well and those who have worked with me in a professional capacity over the years, will affirm that I like looking for metaphors to help make sense of something or to explain a complex topic. In the same way I used a case study to set the stage for this book, I want to use a metaphor to help us visualize and simplify the next step in our understanding of stakeholder expectations.

Consider a traffic intersection created by two roads, heading in different directions and eventually encountering the other. The joining together of two divergent approaches can be a formula for chaos, accident, injury, or worse — unless of course the intersection is managed with assistance. Sometimes that assistance is a human traffic officer, or sometimes it is a mechanical traffic light, or maybe a four-way stop sign.

The image of the intersection connects to the thesis of this book quite naturally. The vehicles are the stakeholders. The road is the business plan and drives the path or direction in which they are headed. The intersection represents the conflicting and competing interests of the stakeholders. And the traffic officer, traffic light, or stop sign are the methods of converting potential chaos into self-preservation and order. As with a literal intersection, the stakes are high as the competing interests within the eco-system of your business are bound to collide. Again, think about surviving and thriving. We want everyone and all parties to find success.

While the vehicles who show up at the intersection may have different expectations, I'm struck by what these vehicles have in common: motor fuel, somewhere to be, and a plan for how to reach their destination. Likewise, we see this with each stakeholder group in this visual overview of what they bring to the table (energy), what drives them (purpose), and how they plan to succeed (intent).

	ENERGY	PURPOSE	INTENT
PARTNERS	Capital	Win	Access to liquidity
SUPPLIERS	Products	Compete	Control the supply chain
EXECUTIVES	Leadership	Accumulate	Optimize financial rewards
MANAGERS	Skills	Advance	Solve business problems
WORKERS	Effort	Getting By	Quality of contribution
CUSTOMERS	Choice	Value	Democratize consumerism
INVESTORS	Talent	Return	Diversify investments
COMMUNITY	Belonging	Preservation	Quality of life

Helping leaders understand stakeholder perspectives and the importance of bringing people together for the good of all parties is a monstrous challenge. However, every now and then something comes along in the world of business that makes the foundations tremble in wonder just a bit. It might be a scandal (Wells Fargo Bank, fake customer account abuse, 2016), a safety breakdown (Boeing, testimony from safety violation whistleblowers, 2024), or a federal regulation (Dodd-Frank, reform of financial institutions and consumer protections, 2010). As I have followed these incredible stories from the world of business, the details largely point to a one-dimensional focus on making money at any cost, further reminding me why the broader stakeholder perspective is so important. If you're still unconvinced, consider this excerpt from the BlackRock CEO letter to shareholders:

> *When my partners and I founded BlackRock as a startup 34 years ago, I had no experience running a company. Over the past three decades, I've had the opportunity to talk with countless CEOs and to learn what distinguishes truly great companies. Time and again, what they all share is that they have a clear sense of purpose; consistent values; and, crucially, they recognize the importance of engaging with and delivering for their key stakeholders. This is the foundation of stakeholder capitalism ... driven by mutually beneficial relationships between you and the employees, customers, suppliers, and communities your company relies on to prosper. In today's globally interconnected world, a company must create value for and be valued by its full range of stakeholders in order to deliver long-term value for its shareholders. (BlackRock CEO, Larry Fink's 2022 Letter to Shareholders)*[2]

When this was published, it created quite a stir. BlackRock CEO, Larry Fink, defied the long-held principle that making money is the sole reason to be in business, that stock price is king, and business leaders should be singularly focused. His entreaty **challenged the notion that the shareholder is the only stakeholder that truly matters**. Fink admonished his CEO peers who have heretofore sub-optomized the role of "employees, customers, suppliers, and communities" — all of whom have a vested stake in the success of business.

This is exactly why I have written this book. I want you to lead your company with the interconnectedness of people groups that Fink is talking about. If you need to, go back and review the illustration of what drives stakeholder behavior (on the prior page). Visualize each stakeholder group within your organization's eco-system and make sure you grasp the energy, purpose, and intent of each group. As I said, the stakes are high.

When a CEO and the leadership team are one-dimensional, bad things happen. When company leaders get focused (in a vacuum) on revenues and operating expenses, the harmony between people groups and what's important begins to fracture.

> [Pharmacy] chains have forced pharmacists to choose between their oath and their job. In California, 91% of chain drug store pharmacists surveyed by the State Board of Pharmacy (in 2021) said they lacked the staff needed to ensure adequate patient care.[3]

Or, when a CEO and the leadership team flexes their power against employees and communities, stakeholders may organize and hit back. A few examples of this include:

- Labor union organizer (and former Amazon employee) Chris Smalls has on multiple occasions referred to Amazon as "the enemy."[4]
- Grocery workers in Seattle criticized their CEO for exercising cost controls aimed at preserving profitability and suggested he take an 80% salary reduction instead.[5]
- Socialist Alternative Party spokesperson, Kshama Sawant, has said that "capitalism needs to be overthrown. We need a socialist world."[6]

I'm guessing you're bewildered by these sentiments. I've always believed that those at the top of the economic pyramid were heroes, role models, philanthropists, patrons of the arts, and good for society. Increasingly, this view (which I would argue was once mainstream) is being replaced by a kind of "revenge activism" that strikes out with venomous vigor at anyone who is wealthy and at any company that has proven to be successful. Such as:

- [As I write this in the year 2024], the wealth and capitalist power class has become the new punching bag in society. Columnist Jon Talton writes about how billionaires are changing America for better or worse.[7] *Worse?* [my comment, my italics]
- A city official in San Bernardino (CA) criticized Amazon for pursuing financial incentives that support its business objectives.[8] *You do understand this is a for-profit enterprise, right?* [my question, my italics]
- On a recent trip to several destinations in Europe, I was counseled by travel agents and other local experts to avoid wearing certain clothing labels, to choose nondescript hotel accommodations and travel in vehicles that do not attract attention. Apparently, these traditional signs of wealth may attract the attention of actors with nefarious intent.

These are examples from the real world that illustrate **intersection chaos** where stakeholders are headed in opposing directions, with competing agendas and wildly different expectations of how you will behave as a leadership team. From where I sit, we either need a traffic cop (governments attempt to play this role, but are largely inadequate and unsuccessful), or we need a better construct to illustrate energy efficiency at the intersections in business.

Behold, the traffic circle. More commonly found in international locations until recent years, the traffic circle (or "roundabout") is less of an intersection and more of an interchange. Traffic continues to flow, at a measured pace, allowing vehicles and their drivers to maintain momentum and continue toward their destination.

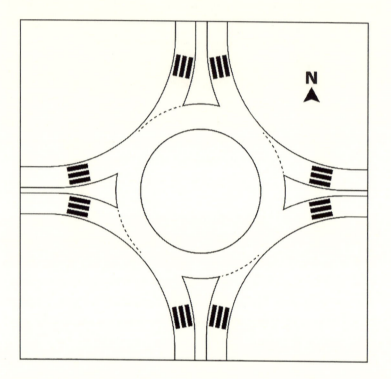

The only real rule is that vehicles waiting to enter the circle must yield to vehicles already moving around the circle. And while traditional intersections are experiencing major safety issues (according to the US Federal Highway Administration, over 50% of traffic fatalities and injuries occur at or near intersections), the traffic circle is a much safer and modern means of managing vehicle traffic for the benefit of all travelers.

So how does this metaphor apply to the reality of stakeholder group chaos? Traditional methods used by business executives to manage the competing expectations of stakeholder groups fail to employ the benefits of the traffic circle. The mainstream CEO today will tell you in no uncertain terms that he/she feels like a traffic cop, using best judgement to grant or deny permission to one group or another intent on pursuing their agenda. It is like all business stakeholders are at a full stop with no movement at the intersection, waiting and hoping for the CEO to give them the green light to proceed. As one moves forward, the others groan in disgust and despair, anxiously waiting their turn for a signal to move forward again in pursuit of their destination.

I discovered this in real time at the Walgreen Company. The CEO was a 30-year company veteran who had come up through the ranks after starting his career as a pharmacist. Many of his executive team had accompanied him up the corporate ladder and felt comfortable approaching him directly for approval or permission on various issues. I got involved when he shared with me his exasperation over the volume of requests for promotions into executive roles, most of which he approved as a courtesy to colleagues he had known for years. When I shared with him internal data indicating that the executive population was growing significantly faster than revenue, profit margin, or any other business metric, he requested my help.

The solution I proposed included two parts: (a) a budget for new executive positions that indexed proportionally to growth in business performance; and (b) a quarterly process of nominating and discussing all proposed promotions with the full executive operating committee. Expectations were created, energy was allowed, progress was made, and destinations were reached — but without the chaos and arm-twisting which created negative energy. It was not a perfect solution for this situation, but it changed the process from an unsatisfactory form of management (intersection) to a more constructive one (interchange).

Here is the takeaway: the stakeholder groups have power; they have competing agendas; they don't necessarily have the big picture; they don't like having to stop at the intersection; and they want you (the CEO, the leadership team) to give them the green light no matter how critical the business may need attention in other areas. The next step in our quest to manage the interests of your business and its stakeholders is to talk about the identification of priorities.

SECTION THREE

Author's Objective: *Equip the reader to be a mature leader who delivers results for stakeholders while also strengthening the enterprise.*

Chapter Seven:

Priorities

As the campus expands, stands of umbrellas — Amazon orange, of course — appear in building lobbies. I assume they're for visitors only until I see employees taking and returning them and no one is telling them to stop, and then the idea that someone somewhere at Amazon spent company money to help me stay dry in the rain comes very close to making me cry. (Kristi Coulter)[1]

At the corner of Royal Brougham Way and Sixth Avenue South in the SODO ("south of downtown") district of Seattle, Washington, just two blocks from the professional baseball and football stadiums, stands a uniformed traffic officer on gameday. This intersection is heavily traveled with vehicles and pedestrians coming from every direction. It is a chokepoint for vehicles exiting from major roadways, attempting to get close to the stadium parking lots. And of course, pedestrians who have parked in one of many off-site parking lots and garages are now walking to the event in eager anticipation of the game.

Putting myself in that traffic officer's shoes, I am wondering if this is a welcome job assignment or not. Standing in the middle of a busy intersection, complete with noise and confusion, exercising judgement on when to allow vehicles and pedestrians their respective right of way, risking personal safety and taking verbal abuse from people who may be frustrated and impatient.

Kind of sounds like the role of the Chief Executive Officer, who many have described as a lonely job. According to Harvard Business Review, "half of CEOs report experiencing feelings of loneliness in their role, and of this group, 61 percent believe it hinders their performance."[2]

Standing alone, with authority, and a target on your back, managing multiple agendas and competing expectations from well-intentioned people wanting what they want when they want it — looking to you for authorization to proceed without interruption. Sounds to me like an exercise in frustration, and almost impossible to resolve. So how do most business leaders go about moving forward in such a challenging business environment? They begin by first determining priorities, which then leads to better informed decision making.

The identification of priorities is most often framed by one or more of these influences: (a) adherence to mission and values; (b) leadership preferences/style; and (c) attention to stakeholders. Let's look at some real-life examples of these approaches to identifying priorities.

There is probably no better illustration of framing priorities out of **adherence to mission and values** than the story of Patagonia founder and CEO, Yvon Chouinard.

> *A half century after founding the outdoor apparel maker, the eccentric rock climber who became a reluctant billionaire with his unconventional spin on capitalism, has given the company away. Rather than selling the company or taking it public, Mr. Chouinard, his wife and two adult children have transferred their ownership of Patagonia, valued at about $3 billion, to a specially designed trust and a nonprofit organization. They were created to preserve the company's independence and ensure that all of its profits — some $100 million a year — are used to combat climate change and protect undeveloped land around the globe.*[3]

You see, Chouinard valued the independence of a privately held company where he could exercise his disregard for conventional business norms. He not only had a passion for the health of the planet, but the mission and purpose of his company was built into the very fabric of their identity. Rather than propagate the hypocrisy associated with leaders who say one thing and do another, he prioritized a legacy of integrity over the accumulation of riches and the luxury of wealth. These were the primary factors that motivated him to give the company away. Whether you agree or not with his intense devotion to the environment, you must admire the radical step of eschewing a massive personal fortune for the sake of a cause he believed in.

My research into the history of mission-driven companies eventually brought me to the story of Walmart founder Sam Walton. A lesser-known fact is that his first foray into the world of retail was to operate a few "five and dime" Ben Franklin franchise stores in the state of Arkansas. From early in his career Sam had a strategy of adopting discounts. Regarding discount promotions, he said, "here's the simple lesson we learned ... by cutting your price you can boost your sales to a point where you can earn far more at a cheaper retail price than you would have by selling the item at a higher price. In retailer language, you can lower your mark-up but earn more because of increased volume."[4]

The Walton business model was rooted in a conviction that discount stores could thrive in small towns with fewer than 5000 residents by selling products as cheaply as possible. After observing the rise of profits and wanting to further build out his collection of retail stores, Walton "proposed that [the owners] of Ben Franklin cut their margins in half, and [they] declined. Sam decided to go it alone, and that's how Walmart was born." (*Business Insider*, February 3, 2011).[5] At the intersection of two competing agendas, adherence to his evidence-based conviction of the relationship between consumer pricing and company profits made it much easier to identify the right priorities for his business.

Not only are priorities framed by an adherence to mission and values, but **leadership style can also have a significant influence on how priorities are identified**. Here is a case in point — how does one even begin to describe the persona and leadership style of former T-Mobile CEO, John Legere? John is certainly one-of-a-kind. He can be zany, off-the-wall, and most certainly unconventional. He can be profane, misunderstood, and difficult to predict. He is well-educated, deeply experienced in the telecommunications world, and a dedicated philanthropist. And without a doubt, he is the most successful CEO in the history of the T-Mobile company, which he helped transform into a global power that competes directly with AT&T and Verizon (competitors he once referred to as "dumb and dumber").[6] Scrolling through the John Legere collection of legendary quotes, we find his simple approach to determining business priorities:

> "The genius of the marketing strategy that we've had in every company that I've ever been in is that if you ask your customers what they want and you give it to them, you shouldn't be shocked if they love it."[7]

Similarly, he said,

> "I don't worry about listening to critics. I worry about listening to customers."[8]

I mentioned that Legere is noted for his philanthropic activity, and this is an important dimension of leadership style. My view of corporate philanthropy goes back to the early days in my career where our team dedicated parts of a business day to helping others in the community. In Portland, we painted the exterior of a youth activity center. In Seattle, we teamed up with company founders to solicit donations from Microsoft employees in support of United Way. In suburban Chicago, members of the Walgreens team participated in a walk-a-thon for the benefit of juvenile diabetes research. I link philanthropy to leadership style for a very important reason: the best CEOs in my experience are those who appreciate the sacrifices others have made, that legitimate needs exist in society, and they are truly compassionate and generous toward those less fortunate. They also make sure their employees can action the same.

Before we leave this notion that leadership style can have a large impact on setting priorities, I must provide a word of caution. Twice in my career I have experienced a derivative of leadership culture I refer to as "kiss the ring." It was where I encountered hierarchal leadership arrangements (some, not all were like this) where company history, inflated egos and longstanding relationships significantly impacted how priorities were set. At Microsoft, some leaders let it be known it mattered little whether you said anything of value, and more of whether you had the pedigree and tenure that would tempt anyone to listen to you at all (fortunately in more recent years, the environment at Microsoft has shifted in a constructive and healthy direction, where the "know-it-all" legacy has been effectively replaced with a "learn-it-all" culture under the leadership of CEO, Satya Nadella, and CPO, Kathleen Hogan). At Walgreens, relationship history, length of service, pecking order and title meant a great deal when it came to establishing business priorities. I recall on one occasion asking a top leader about the goal to eliminate $1 billion in SG&A expenses. While I have had lots of experience driving out costs and was not wimping out at the challenge before us (I was a C-level officer at the time), I never did get a satisfactory answer to how the goal had been determined and what business outcome we hoped to achieve. The answer I did get was condescending and non-responsive.

The third framing of priorities **is influenced by paying attention to stakeholders**. A few years ago, after failing to find a listening ear for redesigning performance management, and then subsequently no interest in my briefing on new trends in equity compensation, it occurred to me that executive leadership at Microsoft did pay a lot of attention to employee sentiment. In those days the company ran an annual employee opinion survey it called "MS Poll."

The poll supplied leadership and managers at all levels with important information about how employees viewed the company. It was in essence an opinion survey, and a sophisticated one at that. This MS Poll team shared floor space with my group in Building 100, and I got to know them and their process very well. To me, it seemed like the poll, though designed and administered by a team with excellent credentials, was missing a few elements we needed to make effective HR decisions, so I proposed exploring employee sentiment using a tried-and-true methodology borrowed from the world of marketing.

We struck up a partnership with Tom Davenport, a senior consultant out of the San Francisco office of Towers Perrin (now known as Willis Towers Watson). Tom and his team had developed a new instrument for measuring employee sentiment built on "conjoint analysis." This survey methodology required employees to go beyond expressing the typical likes and dislikes, by indicating preferences as they were guided to make binary choices and tradeoffs.

The simplest way to understand conjoint analysis is using the illustration of purchasing a new vehicle. Imagine the manufacturer/dealer offers you a choice of two deals: (1) a new car priced at $50,000 with the option of 25 different exterior color choices; or (2) the same new car priced at $48,000 with the option of 3 different exterior color choices. There being no right or wrong answer, the customer gets to choose which deal they prefer, an indication of whether price or selection is a more important aspect of their buying decision. We had a vision that data collected in this manner had the potential for immense value with our leadership team as they sorted through a variety of workforce investment decisions, which had the potential of immense value for our leadership team.

Several thousand Microsoft employees completed the survey, with strong representation by gender, ethnicity, length of service, geography, profession, and business division. The Davenport team educated us on how to view employee sentiment through a unique lens, and we figured out that some of the least costly things to implement were valued as the most influential on an employee's intent to stay. When preference scenarios were posed in the context of employee "intent to stay," employee stakeholders were very clear about what they needed and this prospect of improving talent retention carried the day with top decision makers. This "efficient frontier" was incredibly helpful in determining priorities and making decisions, which we presented to the highest levels of leadership. Now over 20 years later, remnants of these informed decisions (grounded in stakeholder feedback and less dependent on leader-initiated preferences) remain at the company in the form of RSU-based equity compensation, investments in on-site childcare, and cost-sharing of healthcare premiums. We asked, we listened, we studied, and we prioritized decisions in a measured and informed manner. As management expert and prolific author, Ken Blanchard has said, "feedback is the breakfast of champions."[9]

Whether it's because of your adherence to your mission and values, your leadership style, paying attention to stakeholder feedback, or (ideally) a combination of all three, you need to escape the haze of stakeholder expectation chaos and do the hard work of prioritizing your investment of resources. This is how you become a solutions-focused leader who resolves the tensions of competing agendas. We will explore other actions you can take in subsequent chapters.

Chapter Eight:

Affordability of Investing in People

Give me neither poverty nor riches, but give me only my daily bread. Otherwise, I may have too much and disown you and say, "who is the Lord?" Or I may become poor and steal, and so dishonor the name of my God. (King Solomon of ancient Israel)[1]

I find it quite interesting to see how highly educated and experienced advisers, commentators and search professionals have described the job of the CEO. One example, published by an executive search firm itemizes fourteen responsibilities:

1. Plan, develop, implement and direct the organization's operational and fiscal function and performance.
2. Act as a strategic partner by developing and implementing the company's plans and programs.
3. Analyze the effects of long-term growth initiatives, planning, new strategies, and regulatory actions.
4. Perform accurate analysis of financial trends and budgets to help the BOD as well as the senior executives to increase credibility and authority.
5. Implement, improve, and enforce policies and procedures that will increase the financial and operational effectiveness of the company.
6. Establish credibility throughout the organization and with the Board of Directors as an effective developer of solutions to business challenges.
7. Provide expert financial guidance and advice to others within executive leadership.

8. *Improve the planning and budgeting process continually by educating departments and key members of corporate leadership.*
9. *Provide strategic input and leadership on decision making issues affecting the organization, specifically evaluating potential mergers, acquisitions, or partnerships.*
10. *Optimize the handling of banking relationships and work closely with CFO to foster and grow strategic financial partnerships.*
11. *Work with the finance team to develop a solid cash flow projection and reporting mechanism, which includes setting a minimum cash threshold to meet operating needs.*
12. *Act as a strategic advisor and consultant offering expert advice on contracts, negotiations, or business deals the corporation may enter.*
13. *Evaluate the company's financial, operational, and sales and marketing structures to plan for continual improvements and a continual increase in operating efficiencies.*
14. *Mentor and interact with staff members at all levels to foster growth and encourage development among the senior executive team and all staff members.*[2]

Where do I begin to describe how incredibly off-putting and worrisome this is? First, strip away all the fancy corporate-speak and you are left with a few key phrases such as "direct performance" and "implement plans." This is an informed view on the job of the CEO, are you kidding me? Or how about these words, "perform analysis" and "enforce policies." Wrong again. Okay, how about this, "provide expert financial advice," "optimize the handling of banking relationships," and "develop a solid cash flow projection." These functions and disciplines may be important to the business, but in my humble opinion this is **not** the job of the CEO (unless the business enterprise is quite small and has not yet built a diversely skilled executive team).

Come on, don't you have well educated, experienced, and highly paid executives to operate the business, determine strategy, manage fiscal obligations, and oversee compliance? I know you do, so why are these itemized as critical responsibilities of the CEO?

When you burden your CEO with this kind of traditional thinking about the role, and the incumbent believes this is their job — scheduling meetings all day long to supervise and micromanage these company duties — imagine all the important things that will not get done because the top leaders are so operationally and functionally focused.

If this sounds like your experience, let me strongly suggest you make a mindset shift. Instead of thinking of yourself as a people leader or enterprise executive trying to manage a business by getting every detail just right, I implore you to reprogram your mind to think like a masterful investment adviser — one who engineers and directs the application of assets in a disciplined, fair, and efficient manner across the major constituent groups that generates a return. There are three key steps to adopting this investment mentality (which we cover in the next three chapters).

The first is to rethink what we mean when we talk about **affordability**. It wasn't until my mid-thirties, as a young professional making a salary around $30,000 per year, that I began to think seriously about saving for retirement. My employer had a $1 for $1 match that seemed too good to pass up, but it would require setting aside 6% of my paycheck into a 401(k) savings account. My first thought was, I couldn't afford it. My second thought was, how could I afford <u>not</u> to? I decided to make a couple of changes to my spending habits and invest a total of 12% of my salary in retirement savings. One of the best decisions I ever made, and I carried on this tradition for the next 35 years.

As individuals, as employees, and as leaders in business, we are faced with these types of spending decisions all the time. Money doesn't grow on trees, you work hard for what you have, and if you are a fiscally responsible person, you take great care to monitor your expenditures. There is nothing wrong with spending money, so long as it aligns with your personal or business objectives.

Yet in my experience, large businesses with huge revenue streams can act like paupers at times, when they resist investing resources in the people that are so essential to their business. Most companies are wealthy by almost any definition, yet their resistance to investing in human beings is alarming.

Investing in customers (as a stakeholder group) is a very interesting phenomenon to observe. While a business may make it seem like they are investing in customers with loyalty points or shipping convenience, many of these actions are nothing more than self-serving attempts at driving higher revenues and profits.

Take for example the price of ice cream, which for most of my life was available at the grocery store in a half-gallon container. When it became too pricey to charge customers for a half-gallon (64 ounces), manufacturers kept the price the same but reduced the size of the package (48 ounces). Nothing about this says it was an investment in the customer, only a clever disguise to charge the same for less product. You can find the same scenario in many aisles at the grocery store, from breakfast cereal to boxes of snacks in half-empty containers, where you are effectively purchasing packaged air.

Here is a positive example of investing in customers. In 2005, Amazon revealed during a quarterly earnings release that it would no longer collect shipping revenue from customers who joined Amazon Prime (for a nominal fee of $79 per year).[3] The market analysts who followed Amazon were perplexed when it became clear that the company was leaving over $500 million in annual shipping revenues on the table. The stock declined as a result, on the theory that Amazon could not afford to do this, but Amazon moved ahead anyway with the investment in customers — who received exactly what they expected to get. Better value!

Today, Amazon Prime has expanded its value offering to include video streaming, audio music, audio books and a document storage service. It has attracted over 200 million subscribers around the world who pay $139 per year (as of 2023).[4,5] Value for customers. Cross-selling revenue for Amazon. Stronger sales volume for third-party sellers. Increased market capitalization for investors. Higher-value stock compensation for employees. Now that was a terrific investment that the smart guys on Wall Street thought the company could **not** afford.

When we talk about affordability, I want to help you think differently about investing in the workforce. I have spent most of my career influencing my employers to invest in pay, benefits, work environment, training and development, culture, and the overall employee experience. With a few exceptions, a proposal for investing in the workforce is met with immediate (and almost scripted) resistance from finance leadership. On one occasion, my team determined that it would require a $6 million investment to bring salaries to the minimum of our salary range (apparently, some managers thought they were being good stewards by offering new employees a salary below the minimum of a range we consciously adopted). When I asked my team what they were doing to get this approved, they mentioned being stonewalled by the finance managers. (By taking our case straight to the Chief Financial Officer, we found an ally who could see the bigger picture and together we made a good investment decision.)

On another occasion, my team was asked to redesign sales compensation in a manner that created healthy incentives for improved team selling performance. After presenting various designs and proposals, none of them were approved because "it would mean that salesperson pay would rival software developer pay, and we can't afford that" (the company reported earnings that year of almost $8 billion).

Another example was the experience I had touring distribution centers (with more than one employer), where the lack of healthy food options and facilities for basic stretching and exercise was contributing to poor health and on-the-job injuries. We nurtured relationships with respectable vendors who submitted bids to build and operate a cafeteria and workout room, but in the end the cost to implement across the distribution network was considered too expensive. One person on my team sarcastically noted that we seemed more strategically inclined to pay injury claims than pro-actively support exercise health and nutrition.

For some strange reason, employers are more willing to spend millions of dollars each year on the never-ending cycle of recruiting new employees and paying workers compensation claims than they are willing to invest in the people already on the payroll. While almost any finance manager has the skill to perform a cost-benefit analysis on a proposed expenditure for the business, this approach seems to stop at the door of investments in the workforce.

For the reader who may not have experienced this tension between the finance and HR functions in the company, this false narrative of profit versus people is a common circumstance that you are likely to encounter at some point in your business career. To give you some context, let me share this personal experience. For years I have been making presentations to internal groups of managers and leaders, and occasionally I ask this rhetorical question: "why does our company need both the finance and

HR teams to influence where we invest in the business?" By the looks on their faces, most people quickly pick up on the natural tension between finance and HR, but they are not likely to have a good answer to the question. My answer goes something like this: "if finance was left to independently make all the decisions about your pay, they would be highly motivated to offer you nothing more than the minimum wage mandated by law. And if HR was left to independently make all the decisions about pay, every employee would get to set their own salary without any limitation. Now, do you understand the untenable nature of these extremes and why these two very important business functions need to co-exist and collaborate?"

Now, let's go back to our case study which reveals the business logic for an investment in employee development. As the Hanson's Home & Hardware business grew to an inflection point, Ted realized the demand for high-performing store managers exceeded the supply. The towns and small cities where Hanson's typically located a store did not have many experienced retail managers, especially with Ted's high standards. For several months, he contemplated various strategies that would create a pipeline of managerial talent that could be deployed in stores as the company grew. He needed men and women with intelligence, business savvy, a history of connecting with customers and a willingness to learn fundamentals of retail and general management. After consulting with his professor friend (and partner) at Northern Illinois University, Ted worked with his management team to identify high potential talent inside the company who could benefit from exposure to formal business education. Hanson's sponsored dozens of aspiring managers who enrolled at NIU and began to build a portfolio of skills that would translate into success for themselves, the customers and the owners.

At first, Ted and Peggy wondered how they could afford to "send these kids to college," but agreed they couldn't afford <u>not</u>

to if the company was to continue its trajectory of growth and success. Peggy suggested they investigate funding the college initiative with one half of one percent of store revenues, and that is what they did. Seven years into the practice of providing scholarships for part-time learners in business, Hanson's counted over 200 employees who had taken ten or more college course credits. The retention rate of this population exceeded 90%, so they ratcheted up the investment by partnering with NIU to fund and sponsor an undergraduate degree in retail management. By the time the PE firm came along, over 500 potential and aspiring managers had participated in the program with over 100 employees/students earning a Bachelor of Science in Retail Management. This investment surely created a benefit for Hanson's, but also was an important benefit for the community. An idea ahead of its time? Maybe, but was it worth the investment? Absolutely.

As a leader in your company, you need to adopt an investment mindset. It begins by rethinking what is realistically affordable, helping those around you do the same, and embracing the opportunity to take risks for all the right reasons. The better leaders figure out where there is a potential for return-on-investment, and they are resourceful in getting it done.

Chapter Nine:

Repurposing Legacy Investments

Illustration by Gary Hamel.[1]

The story of Nike Golf is a poignant example of how a successful company goes about re-evaluating and repurposing its investments. I learned the inside details of this story by following the social media presence of Jordan Rogers, the ex-Nike Brand Marketing Director. Rogers was quite specific (on Instagram) about the mutual parting of the ways between Nike and golf superstar Tiger Woods, and the impact that decision would have on the brand.

Furthermore, in an interview with Bloomberg News in 2017, co-founder and Board Chair, Phil Knight, revealed that in 20 years Nike lost money on the venture into golf (equipment, balls, apparel, etc.).[2] Jordan Rogers reflected on the decision to get into the game and a groundbreaking endorsement partnership with Tiger Woods, which very few would question then or now. However, in their analysis of the trajectory of Nike

Golf as a profit center, they were also faced with the reality that their "running business" (the sport for which Nike is most synonymous) was incurring more credible competition than it had in decades. The emergence of new stylish and affordable shoes such as those offered by Deckers Outdoor (Hoka) and On Holdings (Cloudmonster) meant that Nike was trending down on the change in stock price (in the years 2021–2023). Nike and Adidas experienced declining valuation, while Deckers and On Holdings were enjoying 40–80% valuation growth.

What did Nike do? They pulled the plug on investments in golf and refocused the dollars and the talent (engineering and marketing) to the "running" space. It's a classic example of repurposing your investment toward the always-important core group of customers.

In my case, after years of proverbial hand-to-hand combat with company leaders over the affordability of investments in the workforce, I changed tactics and began to think and talk in terms of repurposing existing spend. The basic concept here is that instead of incrementally adding new workforce investments to the cost of doing business, thereby shrinking net profit, we aim to keep expenditures flat and engage in a purposeful review for how dollars could be allocated in a more efficient manner. To do this well, and in the language of business, you need to begin by getting educated on your fully loaded employment cost and where it is being directed. In my career, this was an approach that worked well for me time and again.

You know how this works with your own personal finances: when you take the time to dig deep into where the money goes each month, you discover that insurance premiums are too high; or you are reminded of a monthly subscription fee you don't even use; or that the landscaping service cost could be reduced or eliminated if you and your family members spent an hour or two each weekend doing your own yard maintenance. After digging into the details, you find expenditures which can be repurposed next time to fund something you really need, like saving for holiday gifts, buying new cushions for the patio chairs, taking a vacation or making your spouse feel special on their birthday. Your quality of life improves — this is worth doing.

The elegance in this approach is you get more of what you want or need without increasing your total spending. I have experienced many examples in my business career where we took this approach, by exchanging an inefficient expense for the prospect of a more worthwhile investment. At one employer, we stopped reimbursing for personal mobile phones and used those dollars to build and maintain a modern cafeteria offering healthy food choices. At another employer, we halved the employee discount on company products and reused the funds to support a commuter subsidy that became widely adopted. And in another example, we reduced the travel and entertainment costs of multiple leadership meetings per year in exchange for "town hall employee forums" which gave front-line workers access to company leaders and information in a manner they had not experienced before.

Sometimes, this repurposing approach led us down the path of redesigning an existing program (with intended consequences), creating the kind of outcomes that supported our intent of treating employees well and promoting their success. One such example was the elimination of local training budgets (proven to be inefficiently spent, and with little to no behavioral outcomes), in exchange for the adoption of a national training facility and leadership institute promoted, endorsed, and funded by the business.

Another example was the degradation of employee sentiment toward their stock options, which had been awarded at market-based grant prices much higher than where the company stock was currently trading. With data in hand showing that the underwater stock price made it easier for loyal and talented employees to seek employment elsewhere, we abandoned the practice of granting stock options and created an opportunity for underwater stock option liquidity. In its place we began granting full-value shares, and because we also leveraged a more friendly accounting treatment for RSUs, we decreased annual stock compensation expense while also improving employee morale and retention.

So, let me ask, do you know the volume of your annual investment in workforce employment? I was in HR leadership roles for a dozen years before I could get comfortable answering that question with the details. I began to build this domain knowledge by laying out the reasons with my team as to why this was important. After getting them on board, we did a lot of digging to find reliable answers. We had to look in multiple databases, work with outside vendors and cajole folks on the finance team to partner with us. (It helped when we shared the plan was to present our findings to the CFO.)

The next step, after learning **how much** we invested, was to discover **where** it was invested. The majority was in base pay and healthcare, and yet we learned that large investments were also being made in retirement savings, workplace environment, incentive plans, employee assistance and personal conveniences like the commuter subsidy. At Microsoft and again at Walgreens we utilized cutting edge approaches to help us understand employee sentiment and preferences, and how this data lined up with where we had been investing. I shared this approach, and the details of these real examples, with an audience of several hundred business professionals attending a conference in Scottsdale, Arizona. My talk apparently hit a resounding chord, as post-conference feedback indicated it was among the most well received presentations of the week.

Repurposing existing spend is a simple concept that yields tremendous benefits. The Hanson's Home & Hardware team learned this lesson, some might say the hard way. In retailing, owners lose sleep at night over three things that Ted wanted to resolve: (a) inventory loss; (b) the cost of employee labor; and (c) workers compensation claims.

Inventory loss was a category of expense that included things like items broken or damaged after the store had taken possession of those items from the supplier. Improperly stored items would occasionally fall from the shelf and incur damage. Employees who monitored inventory intake would make mistakes counting or documenting properly. Inventory loss also includes "pilferage," or the disappearance of items from inventory — either before or after they reached the selling floor or shelf. Ted's solution? In keeping with the axiom "inspect what you expect," he asked the store managers to randomly audit inventory intake accuracy. He also asked the store managers to occasionally stand just inside the front door welcoming customers as they entered and wishing customers a good day as they exited. This simple idea planted the expectation (in the minds of employee and customer alike) that someone in management was engaged and observing human activity. While this approach cost the store nothing, it did require the manager to repurpose his/her time. And the result? In stores that properly implemented these changes, inventory loss decreased by about 40%.

Cost of labor is a significant expense for a retailer, lagging only behind the cost of inventory by volume of dollars spent. To deliver on his promise of great customer service, Ted had done what so many owners have done — he hired as many good people as he could find. This approach, while defensible in some measure, drove his employment and healthcare benefit costs higher than his competitors. Ted's solution? He began to think about the efficiency of employee labor hours, rather than over-staffing on the operating hours that seemed intuitive to him. For example, he discovered that **eight better-performing employees** could do a fine job of stocking shelves and meeting customer needs, instead of his usual practice of scheduling **ten acceptable-performing employees** who were not as proficient in their jobs. By improving his hiring standards, tweaking the interview process and reinforcing efficiency with occasional training reminders, Ted discovered he saved money on payroll, and had a little margin left over to give his best employees a wage increase.

Worker compensation claims are the result of employees incurring either accident or injury at work. A slip and fall. A muscle or soft-tissue back strain. An illness or skin condition sourced from a chemical or cleaning solution. When these things happen, the retailer is required by law to maintain a record of these incidents, refer the injured employee for medical treatment, and pay for their medical expenses and wages for any time lost from their normal work schedule. When Hanson's was small with only a few stores in business, these claims were rare, and the expense was barely a footnote. However, as the operation grew into multiple locations and multiple states (which have their own unique government regulations around the cost and administration of worker compensation claims), Ted and his team noticed that claims were a growing trend, and the expense was material. Hanson's solution? They created safety teams in every store, made up of 2–3 employees and at least one assistant manager. These teams were charged with proactively fixing potential accident conditions, such as slippery floors or a broken ladder in the storeroom. They made sure that no hazardous chemicals or cleaning materials were being used in areas (like restrooms) where employees or customers would be exposed. The safety teams created friendly contests where stores would compete on the number of days/weeks/months they could sustain an incident-free workplace. Across the network of stores, these actions resulted in a 30% decrease in claims. The solution costs almost nothing to implement, only a vision for addressing it and a few low-cost prizes for the winning store teams.

Here is another example that created a benefit for a community in the immediate vicinity of a residential development project. The financial backers of the development project faced some resistance from residents who were not convinced of the merits of the proposal. There was a vocal contingent of anti-change naysayers, and there were environmental challenges too. However, the most significant resistance came from neighbors who believed they had little to gain from this influx of higher income newcomers to the community.

The stalemate was broken at the suggestion that each new homeowner be mandated to donate 0.5% of the purchase price to a Community Enhancement Fund. The donation would be collected during the home closing process facilitated by the title company, and then remitted to the Fund. The Community Enhancement Fund was chartered, registered, adopted by-laws, appointed a local governance committee, commissioned an annual audit of the books and reported its activity in a report that was published annually and documented in the local newspaper. The results? Seed money for small businesses, college scholarships, modernization of recreation equipment, a renovated skate park, a music room at the local school, sponsorship of a holiday concert and many other worthwhile projects were funded under the banner of community enhancement. I do not know who should be given credit for the idea, but this is a constructive example of repurposing existing dollars for the benefit of community stakeholders.

To become masters at investing in stakeholders, specifically with customers, the workforce and in the community, you need to incorporate the art of **repurposing** into your business investment strategy.

Chapter Ten:

Modernizing for Asset Efficiency

Singapore is a wealthy island city state in South-East Asia. Once a British colonial trading post, today it is a thriving global financial hub.[1]
The Singaporean economy is regarded as free, innovative, dynamic and business-friendly. For several years, Singapore has been the only Asian country with an AAA credit rating. Singapore attracts a large amount of foreign investment as a result of its location, skilled workforce, low tax rates, advanced infrastructure and zero-tolerance against corruption. It was the world's 4th most competitive economy in 2023.[2]

Many people have investments in the stock market, or real estate, or assets like precious metals or other collectible items. If you've been investing like I have over the past few decades, you know that occasionally you need to review your investment approach and strategy to make sure your financial future is secure. The financial instruments of choice have changed over the years to de-emphasize fee-loaded mutual funds and favor alternatives like hedge funds and ETFs.

In my profession, I began to apply this phenomenon, which I refer to as "modernizing" the company's investments. Some things, like store formats, customer loyalty programs, shareholder amenities and employee benefit plans can lose their impact with age. They may over time (as the world around you modernizes) lose their efficacy for retaining healthy relationships with employees, customers, shareholders, and other key constituent groups of people you need to survive and thrive.

At one employer, I inherited oversight of an employee profit-sharing plan, with $5 billion in asset values that was managed in-house. Not only was there inherent risk with this arrangement, but there were also better, lower cost investment and record-keeping alternatives in the financial services marketplace. We made the case, secured approval, conducted diligence with potential vendor/partners, made the switch, minimized the risk and modernized the roles of existing employees to leverage their skillsets (e.g. people analytics, vendor management, finance).

At another employer, we were concerned about the rising cost of employee health insurance. With real costs increasing annually by double digit percentages, and a workforce that was rapidly expanding by over 20% per year, we needed to re-evaluate how we were offering and subsidizing a critical benefit that employees really cared about. Because the largest employment populations existed in middle to large cities across the nation, we contracted with local clinics and affordable care organizations to provide lower cost, high quality healthcare in exchange for driving our significant employee populations to the contracted provider network. Because of this modernized effort, millions of dollars were saved from both company and individual employee pockets — bending the healthcare inflation trend in the right direction.

Why am I using the word "modernizing" rather than the word "changing." This is more than coincidence; it is purposeful for a few reasons. Modernizing has the connotation of keeping up with the times and all the innovation and technology that goes with it. I was recently telling my teenage grandchildren about our home washing machine when I was 6 years old (in the 1950s). No electricity required, it was powered manually by placing an item wet from being drowned in a tub of soapy water and wringing it between two wooden rollers. As I told this story, the puzzled look on their faces said something between "he's crazy" and "he must be kidding."

Change creates anxiety and fear in some people, whereas modernizing has a sense of value that is worth the adventure. Modernizing creates a shared impression that we need to adopt something different, choosing what is new and improved to stay relevant. We modernize all the time, even if we don't realize it as such. We trade in old vehicles for newer ones. We remodel the kitchen, or the bathrooms, or the entire house. We upgrade our job skills by enrolling in a training class or certification course. We choose the technologies of online banking, streaming our favorite content and communicating around the world in live formats of audio and video. Generally, we embrace modernization in many forms.

Modernization in the realm of customer relationships has been incredible. Firms provide interactive smartphone apps for their customers, allowing them to complete a transaction within seconds from the comfort of their home. Family members can engage in board games using electronic devices and compete simultaneously with friends in distant places. Rewards programs are offered by almost every retailer in existence, from the coffee shop to the grocery store to the pharmacy and to the gas station. In exchange for your continued loyalty to their retail brand, you receive points, rewards, discounts, free stuff on your birthday and so much more. For the most part, we accept these forms of modernization without question.

In the world of investor relations and interactions with shareholders, things have modernized as well. Publishing a printed prospectus, annual report or proxy is almost an old school practice of the past, where now many disclosures are handled electronically (where allowed by law). Even the face-to-face annual meeting of shareholders has modernized, whereas in the old days a large convention hall was rented in the headquarters city to accommodate the hundreds of shareholders who came to experience their investment firsthand. They received sample products, walked through aisles filled with exhibits of emerging products and were treated to complimentary food and drink. These folks got to see the Board of Directors, the CEO, and the CFO up close and personal. And yet in many publicly held firms today, the annual meeting experience has been modernized around virtual meeting technology, with less personal exposure but more efficient in time and effort for everyone.

Here is an example of an investment scenario that brings all of these strategies together into a cohesive whole. The members of the private community where we live fund modernization projects all the time, by setting aside a portion of the homeowners association monthly dues into a capital allocation reserve account. Streets get repaired. Older buildings are renovated. Sports courts are resurfaced. Signage is improved. New amenities are introduced. The association can **afford** it because the reserve account receives mandated homeowner contributions each month and therefore exists to fund capital expenses. The leadership has chosen to **repurpose** a small amount each month away from funding short-term cash needs to funding long-term capital improvements. And we love living in a **modernized** community that is attractive and welcoming to new and existing residents. This is simply a smart way of doing business and life.

I urge you to challenge the internal myths about affordability, repurpose existing expenditures into more efficient investments, and modernize occasionally to make sure you remain relevant. That is what the best CEOs and master investment advisers do so well.

Chapter Eleven:

Use It or Lose It

It's like a man going off on an extended trip. He called his workers together and delegated responsibilities. To one he gave five thousand dollars, to another two thousand, to a third one thousand, depending on their abilities. Then he left.
Right off, the first worker went to work and doubled his supervisor's investment. The second did the same. But the man with the single thousand dug a hole and carefully buried the money. (A parable from Jesus.)[1]

As a young man I was taught the principle of stewardship and the importance of wisely using my resources regardless of whether I had a little or a lot. The focus on stewardship led me to this easy-to-remember alliteration, "time, talents and treasure." In this section we have described in much detail what we mean by excelling as an investor when it comes to the stakeholder groups. This investment focus has been almost exclusively on the use of financial assets; however, I would be remiss if we did not cover two other asset classes that every reader and every leader have in bountiful supply. So, let's talk about investing the assets of "time" and "talent."

We all have time, the same amount of time as the person sitting next to you. Leaders who attended Ivy League institutions do not have more time than you. Wealthy venture capitalists do not have more time than failed entrepreneurs. I have spoken to aspiring business leaders who believe they will have more time once they are in a position to delegate to others, but of course this is not true. We all have the same amount of time.

So, what's the issue? Well, people do use their time differently, and some may have a perception of time that may be counter to reality. But for our purposes here in the context of asset investment, I encourage you to utilize your time more efficiently in your relationships across the stakeholder groups. As we have already described, employees and investors may feel more disconnected from company leaders than ever before. You can fix that by taking the initiative to meet stakeholders on their home court. Go to the store. Visit the manufacturing plant or distribution center. Take your lunch in the employee cafeteria. Travel to your best suppliers and thank them for contributing to your success. Take the lead on Analyst Day. Go talk to customers in a friendly and disarming manner. Host a dinner party for your business partners and present special gifts selected especially for them.

We all have talents, skills, abilities, competencies, and professional experiences in some measure which add value to us as individual contributors and leaders. While time is distributed to all of us in the same measure, talents attach to us differently from one person to another. These talents accrue to you based on your heredity, your upbringing, your interests, education, relationships, work experiences and so much more. Each living person has a unique toolkit of talents, and the objective (in my worldview) is to bring those tools to life's work in a wholesome and constructive manner that benefits you, **and** others in your world of influence.

One of my favorite business practices in the corporate world is the "talent review and assessment." The simple idea with this practice is to collect data on employee talents and create an inventory that can be accessed to form teams and get work done, while providing a sense of purpose, fulfillment, and ownership for employees at all levels. Fortunately, there are technological tools available that can help with the process.

However, it begins by inviting each employee to create their own "talent profile," providing a summary of background, interests, and work experiences. Surprisingly, some people are hesitant to participate in this process, which is understandable (in the absence of the company doing a great job of communicating its purpose). What I'm wondering is this: whether you are a business student, a company leader, an aspiring executive, or an accomplished industry icon — do you know with confidence the details of your own talent profile?

Maybe you have experience with diagnostic tools that help you see yourself through the talent lens, like the Myer-Briggs Type Indicator, or StrengthsFinder, or Enneagram Personality Test, or any number of other reliable and respected instruments. What I have learned about myself through these valuable tools is that I prefer working with people versus working with things. My sense of creativity is dormant in isolation, but quite active in collaboration with others. I am better at designing than executing, although under duress I have learned to do both. I am a peacemaker by nature but can deal effectively with conflict when necessary. I generally display good judgement, but can recall many situations where I was duped, naïve, or just plain shallow in my decision making. In my later years, I have curated a bank of experiential learnings that come in handy when advising others who are more junior in their careers. Maybe the most valuable thing I know about myself is that I am eager to see others succeed.

In possession of your own personal bits of self-awareness, you can begin to think how to invest in your unique set of talents. For me, although I loved the general management side of business, focusing on people and employment challenges was a better path for me. I was able to use my background in communication to present important content to large audiences. Coaching top leaders, peers, and subordinates in the science of interpersonal communication became second nature to me. Carefully observing behavioral patterns, understanding what drives and motivates people, and designing systems and plans that increase the probability of success — this is what drove my career in business.

I am also the proud father of four adult children, to whom I have dedicated this book. There is no question they have learned from me over the years, and there is also no question I have learned from them. With their careers in corporate communications, financial services, healthcare, and retail management, we frequently discuss the world of business and how they are experiencing it through their unique lens. You might say we have a family history of mutually investing our time and talent into each other.

In speaking about the theme of this book with my daughter, Jennifer, she nodded her approval on the importance of the stakeholder perspective in her line of work (corporate communications). It has become second nature for her to engage stakeholders by listening to what they care about, asking probing questions, conducting research, and creating a compelling message about the business. The more I thought about her comments in the context of investing your talents in others, it occurred to me that "stakeholder engagement" is a stand-alone skillset that can be nurtured and applied to the people whom you influence and care about.

Another of my daughters, Brianna, is a trained medical assistant. For quite a few years she has been employed by a major health system, in a variety of roles. I recall her telling me about supporting a team of neurologists, and how the appointment schedule on each Monday was dedicated to ALS patients. This is a tragic disease with no known cure. It takes so much kindness, patience, maturity and a caring heart to engage authentically with these patients and their families. It is not always easy to do, but she dedicated her time and talent to terminally ill people whom society at large has pretty much forgotten.

Be present. Invest time. Use your talents and share your experiences for the benefit of others. Show up, authentically. Study, and then leave the PR script on your desk. Be yourself. You are likable. People want to be around you; they want to nurture a business relationship with you. Smile. Converse. Show interest in other people. Say real words. Do real things. Be a real person.

You will not succeed in authentic leadership by only connecting with stakeholders electronically. We still live in a society where a smile and a handshake make a big difference. It requires a purposeful investment of your time and talents to encourage stakeholders that you are all in this together. And if you do on occasion fail to invest wisely, you have lost an opportunity — however, but by the grace of God, you are given a second chance to invest in the very next day.

SECTION FOUR

Author's Objective: *Commission* the reader to lead their organization with confidence by adopting a new personal ethos.

Chapter Twelve:

Decision Time

[In 2022], Starbucks unveiled a company-wide reinvention strategy and continued to deliver on more than $1 billion in investments in retail partners and stores for prioritized areas such as increased pay and sick time accrual, new financial well-being benefits, modernized training and collaboration, store innovation and equipment and the celebration of coffee.
"As a human connection business, we have limitless possibilities to deliver for our partners, our customers, our investors and our communities through every cup and every connection. I am excited to work alongside our partners worldwide to unlock the limitless future of Starbucks." (Laxman Narasimhan)[1]

Earlier, we talked about the value of case study learning. As I think about case studies, I am reminded of my early days in business when I read and re-read some of the best business books of that generation. Examples include *In Search of Excellence* by Tom Peters, *Good to Great* by Jim Collins, and *Competing for the Future* by Gary Hamel.

The case study approach in these books promoted my understanding of business, gave me handles on how decisions got made, memorialized principles from real companies, and positioned me to think ahead about what I might do in challenging circumstances. So, as we enter the home stretch of this volume with its focus on stakeholders within the ecosystem of business, let's walk through a series of decision-making examples that I can speak to firsthand — starting with the Hanson's case study and how the stakeholder perspective is evident in each of these stories.

Hanson's Home & Hardware (HomeSource): Ted Hanson and the business model he created and launched over 40 years ago, eventually growing to be acquired and rebranded as HomeSource, provides a few noteworthy lessons on how to manage the stakeholder groups and their competing interests. The first, and not to be overlooked, is that Ted was a man of integrity, a person beyond reproach. His instinctive and successful manner of building relationships, of drawing people into sharing his vision for how customers could be served, were realities he cultivated from a place of sound character and noble intent. Ted did not set out to find great wealth, nor did he ever dream that his business model would thrive to the extent that others would value it in the billions. Ted chose to work hard, engage fairly with his partners and suppliers, pay his employees generously, invest in management training, share his success with the community and embed a slogan ("yes, we've got that") that gave customers confidence to shop — and come back again.

The second insight to note here is that even as Ted understood and nurtured relationships with all stakeholders, he also came to realize that to survive and thrive in the retail world meant he would have to double down on investments in employees and customers. Poorly trained, disengaged employees doing the bare minimum do not provide a customer experience that serves the best interests of the business. The store managers needed to see advancement opportunity, and front-line workers needed an expectation of job security. Ted made sure there was an intentional focus on career growth by investing in a leadership institute he championed in partnership with Northern Illinois University. And he wasn't content to just pay market median wages to the workers who stood front and center with the customer every day. Even before the concept of a living wage was popularized, Ted voluntarily reduced his own share in the financial rewards of success by setting wages higher than any other comparable retailers in the area.

His commitment to customers also became apparent when he risked the rewards of expanding inventory into the garden center, patio furniture, lighting, and holiday décor. Not all these decisions penciled out to be profit generators in every store, but they sure did strengthen the bonds of customer loyalty that fueled top-line revenue growth, and that became very attractive to future investors. From these examples, you can see evidence that Ted was managing the interests of multiple stakeholders (suppliers, employees, customers, and investors) around the common expectation that Hanson's would not only survive but thrive.

Microsoft (2000–2004): Prior to joining Microsoft as compensation leader for the US business, I had 12 years of HR experience with two smaller companies in the Portland (OR) metropolitan area. I did not have a lot of name recognition outside of Portland, with one exception being a professional association which had accredited me in 1993. So, the outreach from recruiters at Microsoft was both a surprise and a validation of my professional expertise and growing reputation.

Only days after joining the team, I came face-to-face with a quiet panic in the executive ranks. Months before, Microsoft had achieved a new record high in market valuation. However, the year 2000 brought new challenges: an anti-trust action by the federal government, emerging boutique competitors making huge salary offers to our experienced engineers, a declining stock price, and heightened concerns about employee attrition. Steve Ballmer had recently been named CEO to succeed co-founder Bill Gates, and it was turning out to be a rough first year.

The first encounter with Ballmer was my sixth day on the job. He invited my boss and I to his office, where he calmly shared he was in the process of getting Board of Director approval to replicate the most recent stock option grant for every employee, in full. In other words, whatever the amount of stock option value you had been recently granted would be doubled in value overnight with a matching award of stock options.

As business anxiety grew over the months, sleepless nights for Ballmer turned into sleepless nights for me. On another occasion, we were given two weeks to figure out how much it would cost to double the salary for every employee. After careful consideration on where to invest, we came back with a proposal to increase company payroll by less than 10% — not the 100% he envisioned — and with targeted focus on high-performing engineers and salespeople.

A few months after my role was expanded to support all of Microsoft operations globally, I was asked to become part of a team that studied a potential acquisition in Denmark. The company saw an opportunity to deepen the reservoir of product design and software development talent by acquiring a proven winner in the Scandinavian marketplace and strengthen Microsoft's presence beyond North America. This investment, announced officially in July 2002, was the beginning of Microsoft Business Solutions — a key strategic initiative focused on small to medium-sized company customers and led by senior vice president, Doug Burgum (who later became the Governor of North Dakota and presidential candidate).

> *Combining the businesses of Navision, a midmarket leader in Europe, and Microsoft Great Plains to create Microsoft Business Solutions will produce superb business opportunities for our partners and an outstanding array of solutions for our customers. Together, we have the people, products and technologies to bring to life Microsoft's mission of enabling people and businesses around the globe to realize their full potential.*[2]

You know why Microsoft has become such a success story? Because the partners won. Suppliers competed. Executives accumulated. Managers accomplished. Workers were job secure. Customers were delighted with the productivity tools and enterprise solutions. Long-term investors got big returns (the stock has grown from **$27 in the summer of 2002 to $427 in the spring of 2024**). And the local community of Redmond, Washington grew from a sleepy farming community into a vibrant and growing economy that provides employment, housing, recreation, visitor activity, and prestige.

Amazon (2004–2011): When I left Microsoft in the spring of 2004 to join Amazon as the global leader of rewards (remuneration), I had been especially careful to understand what I was getting myself into. Multiple people had been appointed to, and then withdrawn or dismissed from the role. The company was still young, not-yet-profitable, and lacking infrastructure and resources — but with a gargantuan vision for how it would revolutionize the marketplace and the quality of customer service. In my interviews with Jeff Bezos, we covered a lot of ground. He tested my analytical chops. He asked good questions about past failures and what I had learned from those experiences. But it was **his answer to a question I asked him** that was most telling: "so Jeff, I know you have very high standards, you have expectations that the people who work for you have their stuff together and bring their 'A' game to work every day. So how would you like me to respond (in the future) when asked a question I do not know the answer to?" We had a brief exchange about the dangers of "faking an answer," and then he basically said I would be granted one "get-out-of-jail-free card," and from then I was expected to know my business better than anyone else in the company.

The impact of that conversation was a game changer for me. I resolved that when it came to strategies, trends, creative ideas, and implementation of how to use pay, benefits and stock as efficient instruments for both personal and collective success, I would in fact need to become the #1 expert at Amazon. In those first few years, we adopted a new compensation planning model that was simple, unique, and incredibly effective. We invested in software developers (assigned to the HR team) who would build systems and processes that enabled us to make good on what we knew was a unique and elegant design. We socialized rewards education throughout the management and executive ranks with presentations titled, "What We Do and Why We Do It." We built tools for recruiters that reduced errors and inequities when creating job offers to prospective new employees. We built a dashboard that illustrated in real-time how Amazon employees were being paid better than their peers at most other technology competitors.

One day, as I was preparing for an executive presentation with the typical level of thorough attention you might expect, I reflected on the conversation with Bezos during my interview. I knew there was more I could learn about how and where we were investing in the employee experience at Amazon. So, I worked with my team to design a world-wide repository of financial information about our investments in pay, benefits, up-skilling, work environment, conveniences and so much more. We normalized the data for geography and foreign exchange rates. At the end of the project, we had a picture of our total monetary investment in the global workforce, and in a comparative sense, how much top-line revenue was being realized in return for this investment. Thanks to Bezos' high expectations, my drive to deliver something of value, and with my team's diligent effort, we built tools that allowed us to facilitate highly impactful business discussions. For example, at one point during my tenure, we were realizing twelve dollars of revenue for every one dollar of investment in the workforce. We took this basic concept of "return on employee investment" and used it in conversations about entering new markets, acquiring other businesses, and budgeting for revenue growth and new headcount. Zooming out, while we were doing this, the marketers and general managers were building new "online stores"; the operations teams were beating their own expectations with innovative delivery models; the merchandising teams were expanding inventory through third-party sellers at mind-blowing speed; and the Prime team continued to elevate the value proposition for subscribers, solving for same-day delivery in many major markets.

There is an urban legend that in the 1990s Bezos originally approached 60 people to talk about the risks and rewards of investing in his start-up e-commerce bookstore. These included family members, former colleagues on Wall Street, venture capitalists, and angel investors. His ask? An investment of $50,000. Why do I mention this?

Because those pre-IPO partners won, big-time. The suppliers and relatively unknown third-party sellers were in the game like never before, competing. Executives with the best business backgrounds wanted to join Amazon, and if they persevered most of them became multi-millionaires. Managers were assigned big jobs, took on strategically important work (like opening new markets, or capability in new geographies), and worked hard to earn their promotions. The availability of good-paying jobs in fulfillment and customer service centers created employment opportunities in many remote and under-served communities. The company initiated hiring programs for high-school computer nerds, for senior citizens, for cross-country RVers, and for veterans of the military who traditionally find it difficult to enter the civilian workforce.

Consumers won on almost every front, as evident by the growth in customer accounts over the years. And investors achieved record-setting returns. If you purchased Amazon shares when the company went public in 1997, with an initial investment of $10,000, the value of your stake would have grown to $16.5 million 25 years later.³ The efficiency of decisions made by company leaders over those 25 years created a phenomenon of success and unparalleled wealth creation for all the primary stakeholders who placed their confidence in Bezos and the company. What a ride!

Walgreens (2011–2015): Little did I know when I left Amazon to join the Walgreen Company as an executive in the spring of 2011, that I would have a front row seat to one of the most interesting, challenging, and frustrating periods in the 110-year history of the company.

The pharmacy giant Walgreens began in 1901, with a small store on the corner of Bowen and Cottage Grove Avenues in Chicago, owned by native son Charles R. Walgreen. By 1913, Mr. Walgreen had grown the business to four stores on Chicago's south side. By 1934, Walgreens was operating 601 stores in 30 states. After a century in business, the company had over 10,000 locations on the best retail corners in America. With deep roots in midwestern values, giving back to communities, and philanthropy, the company was led continuously for nearly 100 years by three generations of CEOs with the surname Walgreen.⁴ The success of Walgreens was so phenomenal it was featured as a case study example in one of Jim Collins' best-selling books.⁵

Not long after I joined the company, a first sign of leaner times was when leadership decided to push the envelope in contract negotiations with Express Scripts, the largest US pharmacy benefit manager representing millions of Walgreens' customers through their employer health plans. I did not participate in these negotiations, but my role was impacted quite significantly when both sides walked away from a contract renewal, and Walgreens began to prepare for a $5 billion loss in revenue and approximately $1 billion of loss in operating income. The new fiscal year had just begun, and the impact of these financial setbacks was not part of the operating plan approved by the Board of Directors. So, the CFO and finance teams began a surgical process to find $1 billion in cost savings. One of the largest targets being considered was the employee profit-sharing plan which had historically distributed roughly $80 million per year of company profits into employee retirement accounts (this profit-sharing arrangement had been around for years, was governed by a long-standing formula, and was on top of the company match on employee salary deferrals into 401k savings accounts). The logic for suspending the plan was straightforward: (1) the plan provided greater retirement savings contributions than most competitors, and therefore was thought to be dispensable; (2) employees had been told year after year that a $0 contribution was possible (although rare); and (3) the company knew employees would complain, but hoped they would soon get over it. Remember, the opportunity was big: $80 million.

I got wind of the conversations being held to suspend the plan just a few days prior to the executive team meeting where the idea would be presented for adoption. Hallway intelligence revealed this was going to be approved, again because it was a juicy savings opportunity balanced against the unexpected loss of $1 billion in profits. I spoke to several executives that week, who basically told me that after broadly communicating the dire emergency of this situation, employees would just have to understand and move on.

Over the next few days, I collected internal and external data; spoke confidentially to external advisers; gathered my peers and direct reports to let them know where this was headed directionally; and what if anything should we be doing about it. First, we collectively agreed to propose a business solution, rather than be naïve and obstructionist. Second, we felt it was important that representing 250,000 employees, we should be heard before leaders make a final decision.

As I did occasionally on a Saturday morning, I was in the office and on this day cranking through various dimensions of the issue at hand. I looked out my window, across the courtyard, and saw a light from the corner office of the CEO. I gave Greg Wasson a call, asking to come over for a brief conversation — and he agreed. In summary fashion I shared my perspective, asking to be heard at his regularly scheduled Monday morning meeting. He generously agreed to give me 30 minutes to make my case with the senior leadership team but cautioned me that from his read of the situation, suspension of the employee profit-sharing plan would be approved. You see, leadership was facing an intersection of competing interests from a key supplier, tens of thousands of managers and front-line employees, and major institutional investors — not to mention the expectations for executive compensation payouts (remember, incentive targets had been set believing the Express Scripts contract would be renewed).

The following Monday, I was invited into the meeting and cordially welcomed by senior executives in the room. Greg sat at one end of the long conference table and I sat in the only vacant corner seat about 30 feet away. Greg briefly shared the story of my visit to his office two days before, and that he thought I should be heard before the group made a final decision on the future of the profit-sharing plan. Then, he gave me the floor.

Guest presenters at this meeting, 99 times out of 100, would open a PowerPoint presentation and begin to make their case. I took a different approach, without anything visual on the screen, saying to the group: "what if I told you we can save the plan, eliminate $80 million of profit-sharing expense if we don't meet Wall Street expectations, remain competitive compared with industry peers, stay compliant with all IRS and DOL guidelines, and communicate to employees with a spirit of transparency and empathy." And then I paused, waiting for leaders in the room to respond. Greg (the CEO) quickly jumped in and stated that if we could wave a magic wand and get all that done, he was eager to hear the details. Other heads nodded in agreement, and only then did I flip on my PowerPoint presentation. I walked them through the specifics, and they agreed to support my proposal. We dodged a bullet and 60 days later we (myself and a long-standing senior person on my team) were in front of over 1000 company leaders in a Dallas, Texas hotel ballroom telling the story of how we saved the plan and what employees could expect with a new profitability threshold in place. But not everyone was cheering. The stakeholders who lost out that year were executives who saw sub-par cash incentive payouts, and customers who were inconvenienced by the exclusion of Walgreens from the Express Scripts pharmacy network (several years later, the two companies came to an agreement and customers were overjoyed).[6]

Advising-Consulting (2016–2023): With a limited amount of career intention, my wife Carol and I moved back to the Pacific Northwest where we had a custom-built home and a wonderful community of family and friends. To stay in touch with my professional network, I sent an email informing people we had relocated and looked forward to easing into retirement. Within a month of that communication, I was invited to meet with CEOs like Kevin Oakes (Institute for Corporate Productivity), Jeff Vincent (Laird Norton Company), and Ted Tanase (Ensocare) to discuss how I might be able to coach and advise them and their partners through some unique business challenges and opportunities. These initial conversations led to others, with independent director Tom Vacchiano at JM Huber, independent director Denny Metzler at Dacor, investor Andy Dale at Montlake Capital, Board Chair Bret Snyder at WL Gore & Associates, CEO Larisa Goldin at Seattle-based Dream Clinic, CEO Gail McLendon at family-owned McLendon Hardware, Nikola Motor investor Steve Girsky and Peloton CPO Mariana Garavaglia.

As I continued to engage in these conversations, a very interesting set of business challenges rose to the surface. In some cases, it was a need to modernize board governance; in others it was about the next generation of proprietorship and whether it made sense to engage with potential buyers. Several of these companies anticipated a CEO transition, due to impending retirements of legacy leadership, and wanted assistance creating a process that would lead to orderly succession and the continuation of business success. I recall helping to interview and then provide coaching to several executives new to the company and/or the role. In another example, I helped launch two new products designed to support and strengthen the maturity of leaders who had been identified as "readiness candidates" for future opportunities.

Thinking back on these experiences, what interests me most is that these engagements focused on improving the business relationship with existing stakeholders. The "aha moment" usually came about with an independent director or CEO observing the need to improve a stakeholder experience and choosing to invest in that stakeholder relationship by engaging an external and independent voice (me) to provide context, perspective and counsel. In the work we did together I can see a link to the leaders, the overseers, the employees, the members, the customers, the investors, and the community.

A word of caution and perspective about external advisers. Conceptually, engagement with independent and experienced professionals is a worthwhile venture. My experiences with consultants over the years in business shaped how I conducted myself with my own clients during this eight-year period. I resisted the temptation to view the engagement as a purely commercial arrangement; in fact, I set my fees on the low side of competitive and offered to refund fees if a client turned out to be dissatisfied (no client ever requested a refund). When I believed that my services were not a good fit for what the client needed, I referred them to someone else. I refused to monopolize time with leaders simply for the purpose of educating myself about their business, believing I should do this on my own time. I preferred to invoice a client based on an agreed retainer for completion of work, rather than progressive billing on an hourly basis. These are examples of the ethics I brought into my advisory practice, however not all external consultants are governed by these principles, no matter how well-intentioned they may be.

As we bring this chapter to a close about how you make decisions in a world of competing stakeholder agendas, I think it is important for you to hear what I am **NOT** saying:

- Outside experts are **not** always in the best position to influence your decisions.
- You should **not** make large stakeholder investments without expecting a return.
- Do **not** over-emphasize how you compare to other organizations.
- Do **not** be tempted to always anchor your decisions on "best practices."

What I **AM** saying to you:

- **Diligently** improve your command of data and the efficiency of stakeholder investments.

- **Confidently** lead your organization into reasoned business discussions on how and where to invest in people, embracing their competing agendas.
- **Boldly** become a team of cost-benefit and expense trade-off gurus.
- **Expertly** link stakeholder investments to short and long-term business value.

Chapter Thirteen:

The Sauce

The real act of ... building a friendship or creating a community involves performing a series of small, concrete social actions well: disagreeing without poisoning the relationship; revealing vulnerability at the appropriate pace; being a good listener; knowing how to end a conversation gracefully; knowing how to ask for and offer forgiveness; knowing how to let someone down without breaking their heart; knowing how to sit with someone who is suffering; knowing how to see things from another's point of view. (David Brooks)[1]

Many books written about the world of business make a well-intentioned attempt at providing a glimpse of the author's "secret sauce to success." I have been thinking about this for years, wondering what secret sauce recipe I might put out there when the time was right. Researching the origin of this phrase "secret sauce," we find the term refers to "a secret element, strategy, procedure, etc., that accounts for or increases the chances of success."[2] My interpretation of secret sauce in the context of this book about stakeholders in the eco-system of business will reference three key behaviors: **collaboration, connection, and courage** — drawn from my decades of experience in and around business leaders.

This sauce is not a secret. Or, maybe better said, the ingredients are not a secret. They are well-known to us, especially if you are a leader in business and you pride yourself on keeping up with the latest trends and academic research. But my hope is that you will see something new, different, and helpful about how these three behavioral ingredients — collaboration, connection, and courage — may be combined into a recipe for your success.

Dr Rob Cross is a professor, researcher, published expert on **collaboration** in the workplace and my former colleague at the Institute for Corporate Productivity. Rob has a distinguished career studying social networks inside organizations. He and his teams use scientific research methods to collect reams of data that illustrate patterns in how people do, and do not, work together for the good of the business. From his writings and lectures, we see that when many organizations describe themselves as "collaborative," Rob finds something quite different when it comes to organizational culture: (1) *participative behaviors* (instead of genuine collaboration, this is an overwhelming focus on group-think and consensus-driven decision making); (2) *hierarchal behaviors* (where even if collaboration is encouraged and innovation is valued, it all comes back to the leaders who hold all of the power and take all of the credit); and (3) *intimidation behaviors* (where employees don't speak up, they don't feel valued or respected, and they have witnessed examples of managers rudely shutting down ideas that do not fit their view of the world).[3]

True and genuine collaboration is another type of behavior altogether. I remember years ago, as the HR manager of a hotel with 300 employees, part of my job was to nurture and support a safety culture in the workplace. A safety culture is not only good for employees, but it also contributes to a positive experience for guests (customers). I recall a conversation with my general manager, wondering aloud how one person (me) could make that happen. I could see the benefit of a safe workplace, but frankly it was far down the list of priorities for other employees who already had many things on their plate. A colleague suggested we start a safety committee, so we did. We selected several managers, but most of the members came from the hotel departments where our data showed that safety was an issue (e.g. housekeeping; restaurants; transportation; maintenance; etc.).

For the first few meetings, less than 50% of the safety committee members attended and many of them came late. It was difficult to get any momentum going; it was obvious that people weren't making this a priority, nor did they see any benefit to themselves personally. One day I was in the hotel gift shop chatting up the manager when I noticed a full box of candy bars and it hit me. The new protocol for our safety committee was born: if the members arrived on time for the meeting, they received a complimentary candy bar. This positive reinforcement began to have immediate results. The members came on time, attendance improved (up to nearly 100%), and they began to engage around the mission of safety. They created contests. They took responsibility for their own work area. They took pride in reducing the number of incidents year-over-year, and hotel management threw a party with some of the realized savings. What makes this a good example of genuine collaboration? Diverse experiences coming together. Finding a way to get people engaged. And sharing in the success.

Much later in my career I was asked by the CEO to form a committee tasked with a humane approach to job reductions and layoffs. Not my favorite thing to do, but I appreciated the intent to at least be respectful and honorable about a process that was necessary, albeit uncomfortable. As executives, our instinctive reaction in a situation like this is to recruit a team of other leaders. However, in this case, I felt it was most important to get the right skillsets in the room, regardless of title and level. We brought together internal subject matter experts from recruiting, people analytics, employment law, benefits, customer service, retail field operations, finance, and corporate communications. To be honest, the launch of our committee was a little rough around the edges. Most of these internal experts had never been in a room with so many diverse skillsets before, and you could tell from their apprehension they found it awkward. Also, they presumed they were there to comment on the process according to their expertise, when in fact what we wanted was a completely new solution to this old uncomfortable business reality. On the practice of substituting traditional business executives with leaders who have technical expertise, Mary Barra (CEO of General Motors) shares this nugget of wisdom:

> We went back to really empowering the individual who knows every aspect of that vehicle and knows every trade-off they've made to get a great vehicle on the road. So, every vehicle has its own chief engineer, and it's single-point accountability ... I have seen a real transformation in just the short few months since we've made that change, in the sense of ownership and the commitment. Before we had some confusion as to who was really accountable and who was making the call. There's no confusion now.[4]

I honestly do not know how any business leader can function in this day and age without genuine collaboration. There is a high probability you are **not** the smartest person in the room, and therefore you need the wisdom of multiple counselors. Furthermore, this generation of business talent wants and needs to be included in the sensitive and impactful deliberations that focus on your ability to survive and thrive. Collaboration is not optional, at least not in this recipe for success.

The second ingredient of **connection** became part of my life organically. After living in northern Indiana for my first four years, our family of origin moved the household six times in the next ten years (from Indiana to South Dakota, to Idaho, to Oregon, to Texas, to Massachusetts and finally to Oregon again).

New schools. New teachers. New neighborhoods. New friends. New churches. New teams. New possibilities. New dangers. New everything.

Human connection would become a highly valued necessity for me. And I did my best to make the most of these connections. Former teachers would become advisers. Former classmates would become co-workers. Former neighbors would become travel partners. Former churchgoers would become soulmates. And when it came time to ask a favor, share a prayer request, express appreciation, host a meal, send a donation, communicate in confidence, or demonstrate care through acts of kindness, it was this connected network of people that became a support system for the quality of my life.

Sometimes these connections lay dormant for a number of years. Recently I had opportunity to revisit a friendship with the valedictorian of my high school graduating class. Kelly graduated from Harvard, got into high-value consulting, returned to Harvard for an MBA, made an impact in the healthcare industry, acquired a business, got involved in a philanthropy serving disadvantaged children in Peru and is the proud "papa" of four adult children and three grandchildren. I was as eager to hear him tell his life story as he was to hear mine. We reconnected. We rediscovered values in common. We enjoyed the conversation. And it won't be long before we connect again. This example of human connection brings me joy.

I have a good friend who is the leader of a not-for-profit charitable organization in a small regional community of about 5000 residents. With assistance from a core group of dedicated and loyal followers, they had launched their mission with some success — but faced the challenge of poor visibility in the community. My friend received advice from marketing experts, other charitable organization leaders and even a few friends. After giving it some thought, he decided to walk the main street in town and introduce himself to every business owner and customer he encountered, and as a former football player, with a gregarious temperament and infectious personality — he is hard to miss. This strategy of connecting personally with people on Main Street worked to his advantage, because after a few months the organization doubled its membership and is now partnering well with other business interests in the community.

Professionally, I've observed many examples of leaders in the business community who did not seem to share my opinion about the value of human connection. The closer a person gets to the top of an organization, the smaller is their circle of genuine and constructive human connection. (I am referring here to the frequency, breadth, and depth of connecting with other people in business because you value the mutual contribution you bring to each other as leaders, not the size of the network of acquaintances which may be significant, but largely ignored.) Many leaders I know are chained to their calendars and the few faces who make a regular appearance. If you question this assertion, maybe you should conduct an informal self-examination: not counting your executive assistant, chief of staff, Board Chair, or leaders of finance, HR, or law, how many other people are you spending time with at work? I would **like** to presume you occasionally connect with Wall Street analysts who follow your company, with investors who attend the annual meeting, with customers at a designated event (even with disgruntled customers who engage with you randomly), with community leaders who are counting on your continued success, and with fellow executives, managers, and front-line employees at various forums for communication and conversation. If you are not doing these things, you are missing out on the value of human connection that keeps you grounded as a leader and in touch with stakeholders who can become your best advocates or your strongest opponents if you avoid them altogether. Do you put yourself out there, or are you hesitant to genuinely connect with people?

Ryan Jenkins, author of *Connectable: How Leaders Can Move Teams from Isolated to All In,* told *Fortune* Magazine that "CEOs can be constantly surrounded by people and still experience loneliness ... after all, the higher you climb the corporate ladder, the more responsibility and stress rests on your shoulders to make decisions as an individual rather than as a team."[5]

The *Fortune* dialogue with Jenkins goes on to suggest that even CEOs of some of the most prestigious companies admit that being in the top seat is an isolating experience. Apple's Tim Cook said being CEO is a "lonely job," and Airbnb's Brian Chesky frequently said that his rise only perpetuated his loneliness. "I started leading from the front, at the top of the mountain, but then the higher you get to the peak, the fewer people there are with you. No one ever told me how lonely it would get."

So, if a leader feels lonely, executive coaches are likely to suggest sharing the experience with a partner, mentor, or trusted colleague. "Loneliness isn't shameful; it's a signal," says Jenkins, who works to create innovative ways to improve employee connection and engagement, including practicing emotional vulnerability. "CEOs shouldn't be ashamed of loneliness but view it as their innate reminder that their influential presence matters to others."

From my earliest days in corporate America, I created opportunities for business travel to various locations and informal conversations **to be present** with employees at all levels. Sometimes it was in a conference room over cookies and milk (people love simple pleasures). On other occasions it was in a distribution center exploring the opportunity to improve worker safety, or to witness first-hand the lack of access to nutrition in the cafeteria/break room. Often, my travel took me to a different geography or continent where local customs, work standards, technology glitches, and commuting hazards were top of mind for employees. These were all invaluable points of connection that made me a better and more empathic leader.

Not to ignore our paying customers, I have found many ways to engage with these stakeholders over the years, as well. Recalling a few examples, I was asked to take part in a customer advisory forum that stayed in existence over several fiscal years. I accompanied operations teams on visits to retail locations, where we informally engaged with customers to let them know we were there to listen and improve their experience. I have been a manager-on-duty, primarily meeting the needs of guests who requested assistance. I have attended trade shows, meetings with customers and prospective customers interested in our line of products and the history of our company. I have met personally with shareholders, with Wall Street analysts, and with activist investors who voiced how they would like our company to operate. And I have for years been involved with recruiting events at top schools and universities looking for long-term placement partnerships that benefit their finest students. Connection is core to the intersection between important stakeholders like these and your business.

In an earlier chapter, I referenced the former CEO of T-Mobile, John Legere. Here is an example of how John prioritized his time to create a human connection with call center employees:

> *We've got about 18 major call centers in the US, and before I was CEO, I heard that no CEO had gone to physically visit them. I go in, or they meet me outside, we take selfies as I stand like a piece of furniture, I tell them about how things are going — but most importantly, I say thank you and help them see that their behavior and their work has driven the culture of the company that's changed the industry and the whole world. It's a bit of a love affair.* [6]

Finally, we have the ingredient of **courage**. Let's be honest. How often do we think about courage as an essential ingredient to business success? You can find ubiquitous references to leadership attributes such as intelligent, visionary, strategic, analytical, operational, confident, passionate, decisive, discerning, and driven — long before you will see mention of courage. (There are some exceptions.) If courage is truly an "unmentionable," one theory to explain it is the strong corporate current of only speaking things out loud that are publicly acceptable.

> CEOs are afraid that speaking out might not only have a detrimental effect on their company's revenue and prevent access to new territories and markets but also that what they say will be used against them.[7]

Internal friction? Poor financial performance? Leadership attrition? Culture clashes? Difficulty with succession planning? Operational misses? Customer dissatisfaction? Safety issues? Nope, unmentionables. The theory is that none of your stakeholders want to hear about such things, even if it is truth. No courage required.

Interestingly, business leaders may be no more likely to undervalue courage than any other population in the eco-system of business. However, the hesitation or resistance by leaders to embrace courage has implications on the organization's ability to survive and thrive.

> The reality is most CEOs often have fierce resistance and put blame elsewhere when trust and engagement are below what they would like. As a result, they are unknowingly slowing their own organizations down and putting a limit on how much progress can be made. As one of our Best Companies

CEOs recently shared: "It took me three years to realize I was the problem and my leadership team needed work."[8]

Each year, *Chief Executive* Magazine uses a selection committee to name "CEO of the Year." Some of the best-performing, high-character men and women in business have been recognized by the publication over the past few years, including Ed Bastian (Delta Airlines), Marc Benioff (Salesforce), Kenneth Frazier (Merck), Brian Moynihan (Bank of America), Arne Sorenson (Marriott International) and Marilyn Hewson (Lockheed Martin).

Recently, the committee provided a sneak preview into the selection criteria, that is on point to our conversation about the importance of courage:

Courage is always a big criterion because it is one of the things that really separates the best of the best. It speaks specifically to the ability to make tough decisions, to put not only the company, but the CEO's job, reputation and legacy, on the line — often without much of a safety net.[9]

I appreciate this reference to the notion of "safety net," as it very simply illustrates the risks associated with courage. When newly appointed CEO, Tim Wentworth, slashed the Walgreens company dividend in 2024, he ended a 90-year streak of quarter-over-quarter dividend growth to shareowners (that's 360 consecutive calendar quarters!). Wentworth said the cut "reinforces our goal of increasing cash flow, while freeing up capital to invest in sustainable growth initiatives."[10] This CEO made a courageous decision to do something that no prior CEO named Walgreen, Jorndt, Bernauer, Rein, Wasson, Pessina, or Brewer had done. He accurately assessed the business is in real jeopardy, and with this one courageous action signaled that Walgreens could no longer conduct business as usual. To me, he is saying, "we are in survive and reset mode, with more change to come." If he is the leader we all hope he is, Wentworth will continue down this path of courageous action, carefully examining the business model and each of the major stakeholder expectations to determine the best push forward to "survive and thrive."

- **Collaboration**, an <u>approach</u> that requires discipline and a belief that every person in the eco-system of business has something constructive to contribute.
- **Connection**, an <u>action</u> that counteracts loneliness by reaching out proactively to people who have a vested interest in your business, and intentionally creating interchange of ideas where conversations happen, energy flows, and common ground is established.
- **Courage**, an <u>attribute</u> that is rooted in the instincts of human nature to survive, to endure, to thrive and to regenerate. "Successful leadership requires many outstanding traits — but courage is the 'mother' attribute. Without it, all else fails." (Doug Conant)[11]

One Approach. One Action. One Attribute. In equal parts, this is the sauce.

Chapter Fourteen:

A New Personal Ethos

Insecure people always need to be heard. They aim to prove their knowledge and feel important. They seek status by getting attention.
Secure people are happy to listen. They want to improve their knowledge and make others feel important. They earn respect by giving attention. (Adam Grant)[1]

For parts of the past four decades, I have been able to observe, evaluate, facilitate, and sponsor both formal and informal performance reviews. In some cases, this was a review of a vendor, supplier, contractor, gig worker, or consultant. In other cases, the review centered on members of my own team, department, or division. In many cases, the review was focused on key talent across multiple roles, often including the job performance of leaders at all levels.

It has always been an accepted presumption that to be successful in business, you needed to demonstrate mastery in the science of business. Here would be a good place to pause and recall that Ted Hanson, prior to opening his first store, had very little exposure to the science of business. He did have character, a solid reputation in the community, an idea and the inner composure to pursue step after step (in consultation with others), leading him to a measure of success he never dreamed of achieving.

You may be wondering what happened to Ted and Peggy Hanson after the company was sold and new ownership came onto the scene. After successfully managing two jobs, Ted retired from the local fire department in the year 2000 and dedicated himself completely to the HomeSource business. Once the PE transaction was completed over a decade later, the Hansons completely retired from their business pursuits and entered a new chapter of life. The proceeds from the sale of the company allowed the formation of a philanthropic foundation, with Peggy Hanson as Board Chair, which invested in pre-school education, emerging entrepreneurs and third-world experiences for people with a heart for global citizens at risk. A major gift to Northern Illinois University and the retail management study program resulted in the college naming endowed scholarships after Ted and Peggy Hanson.

On many occasions Ted was a guest lecturer in NIU classes, and he became a strong and public advocate for the value of education and trade experience for high school graduates. He was a commencement speaker, a mentor of young entrepreneurs and a coach of his own sons as they built their careers in the family business. Peggy was a prolific volunteer with the local chapter of United Way, a strong supporter and donor to Young Life (a Christian ministry to middle and high school students) and a mentor and role model to her grandchildren.

Why am I giving you this level of detail? Because I want to make the point that financial success and building generational wealth was not the goal nor was it the end game for Ted and Peggy. Their objective was much more noble, and more enduring than the accumulation of assets. They wanted to contribute to their community, make a difference, give back and serve as role models of character, perseverance and integrity for a new generation of citizens. They discovered a new personal ethos and their legacy is on display to this day.

In general terms, there are foundations, nomenclature, best practices, time-tested principles, and a body of knowledge that all contribute to the science of business. In tandem, without a doubt, there is an expected level of intelligence and cognitive adherence to the science which can be studied, learned, and demonstrated. In talent and performance review terms, we wonder aloud whether the person being reviewed is "smart" and wish we had tested them for IQ.

However, in recent years, the term "EQ" has also become part of the conversation as a measure of talent not typically measured by the IQ assessment. Emotional intelligence (EQ) refers to the person's grasp of interpersonal skills, the ability to control their emotions in trying circumstances, the perspective one may need to see all sides of an issue, or the attributes of personal charisma that makes other people want to follow. However, EQ is defined less scientifically than IQ, measured more subjectively, and certainly much more open to interpretation. In fact, at times in my career during a certain performance review discussion when EQ is thrown around casually, it has been clear that not everyone in the room has a common understanding of what it is, or why it's important.

Not long ago, I stopped using the term EQ and substituted a concept that feels more tangible and less esoteric. I like asking myself, "is this person a **mature** leader?" I find it easier and more helpful to engage in the answer to that question. So, as we wrap up, here is my 5-point hack for thinking about leadership maturity:

1. **Mature leaders are not easily offended.** Mature leaders have perspective on a variety of issues and concerns facing the enterprise and they remain composed even when things do not go well. Conventional wisdom says, "everybody is a critic," however this usually doesn't faze the mature leader. Maintaining perspective, retaining focus, empathizing with the offending party and offering real solutions that neither disrespects nor ignores legitimate feedback from engaged stakeholders. In the face of opposition, maturity is a prerequisite.

2. **Mature leaders delegate to others for business strategy and operational excellence.** Contrary to the poorly designed CEO job description we noted in an earlier chapter, the mature leader acknowledges the risk of micro-managing the miniscule details of the business. Otherwise, managers can become co-dependent, executives robbed of valuable time, and inertia sets in when people are not functioning properly in their roles. It takes maturity and courage for the leader to step up and say, "I support you, I will advocate for you, and I will coach you — however, I will not do your job for you."
3. **Mature leaders focus on nurturing key stakeholder relationships in the eco-system.** Because partners, employees, customers and investors (and boards of directors) tend to build relationships in your company based on hierarchy (in my experience, this is still very prevalent), they want to see, hear from, and speak with the Chief Executive. Don't get me wrong, they like getting to know the depth of executive talent around the CEO and how these individuals might be positioned as CEO-material in the future, but this is not a substitute for formal and informal dialogue with the CEO that digs deep into the short-term and long-term strategic issues for the business. Leaders who choose (intentionally, or unintentionally) to under-invest in these relationships do so at their peril. In my presence on one occasion, the CEO was asked in a town hall meeting why he repeatedly spoke about the interests of shareholders, but rarely mentioned the welfare of employees. Ouch.
4. **Mature leaders stay focused on what is important, avoiding constant distractions.** You may recall the Seattle police officer directing traffic at a key intersection on gameday — this is the picture of staying focused

and unfazed by distractions which (without mature leadership) can quickly degrade into pure chaos. It takes incredible discipline and demonstration of deep maturity to remain focused on the important, resisting the temptation to become occupied and tormented by the urgent. I suggest you empower your executive assistant or chief of staff to keep you focused on the high-leverage issues and stakeholder relationships with the most impact on your success.

5. **Mature leaders are world-class investors.** Former Cisco Systems CEO, John Chambers, was in the corner office for 20 years from 1995–2015 and built Cisco into a technology powerhouse with annual sales growing from $1.9 billion to $49.2 billion (an incredible story). Chambers was the architect of Cisco's growth strategy based on investment focus on acquisitions. What is he doing today (after retiring from Cisco)? He is the founder and CEO of an investment firm helping disruptive start-ups across categories and geographies. World-class? The results speak for themselves.

If these traits do not seem new to you, and if this maturity ethos accurately describes how you manage and lead in business, you are to be admired and appreciated for your choices. However, others may find this definition of maturity to be off-putting and contrary to how you operate. To you, I offer this incredibly wise statement by Oprah Winfrey: "the greatest discovery of all time is that a person can change his future by merely changing his attitude."[2]

In closing, to those of you who lead us in the pursuit of business excellence, in a complex and risky economic environment, we need you to be a mature leader who actively resolves the intersection chaos that exists because of competing stakeholder expectations. We need you to step up with more grace, more humility, more empowerment, more high-value connection, more courage, and more value-driven investment in the people with whom you partner on your mission to survive and thrive.

Whether you are a student in business school, an entrepreneur, a team manager, a company leader or named executive, it is so important that you see stakeholders as the "bread of life." The imperfect, well-intentioned, engaged and invested human beings who serve as your stakeholders want and need you and your firm to survive and thrive. The very foundations of capitalism in America (in the best sense of the word) rely on your ability to orchestrate these disparate parties into a harmonious symphony of organizational and purposeful achievement. This is an exhortation to see people in business differently than you have before; less as an obstacle, less as an orthogonal distraction intersecting with your business, and more like cohorts of people with whom you interact, interchange and invest.

My hope is you will heed this call to action, to nurture a new and modern personal ethos of mature leadership that values diverse stakeholders, and that you will invest the assets of time, talent and treasure in the people contributing to the success of your business.

Author Notes and Acknowledgements

After a full career spanning parts of four decades in the corporate world and another eight years advising companies and coaching leaders, the next chapter of my professional life is a pre-occupation with writing. There are many things about taking on writing projects that I find satisfying, including the incredible opportunity to connect with people I respect and trust to read my work and give me feedback. For this treatment of *Stakeholders*, it was important to receive feedback from diverse perspectives and from people who were steeped in the kinds of business topics we cover in this book.

Dr. Marshall Goldsmith made my day when he agreed to read the manuscript and write a Foreword to the book. I met Marshall in Chicago more than a decade ago and we made a connection (sound familiar?). Not only does he continue to write, coach and speak to audiences all over the world, he is a respected thought leader who contributes to our shared association with the Institute for Corporate Productivity. It is amazing to be counted as a colleague and peer among talented *i4cp* leaders and authors such as Kevin Oakes, John Boudreau, Mark Blankenship, Pat Wright and others.

My sincere thanks to board advisor and executive coach **Steve Welch**, a former CEO and CFO who now serves on the board of directors of the Lease Crutcher Lewis construction firm. Steve's mastery of business principles, his attention to detail and the deliberate manner he communicates with distinction has been incredibly helpful in making *Stakeholders* a valuable read for anyone wanting to learn more about business.

Many of the early readers I asked for feedback are former members of my teams. **Kristie Provost-Gorman** is a name I heard about in my first couple of years at Walgreens and then came to work with her directly on a few projects before she was appointed to my staff team. If you can imagine combining extraordinary analytics, dogged determination, captivating communication skills and the personality of a saint into one incredible human being — that is Kristie. After Walgreens, she spent a few years as a principal with PwC and is now leading the compliance and privacy disciplines at Option Care. With everything on her plate professionally and personally, she welcomed the opportunity to read the manuscript and spent hours with me deliberating over how it could be improved. Her feedback was awesome!

Randy Fox is a former operations and sales executive in the printing industry and former collegiate basketball referee; he has been a family friend for close to 15 years. After his upbringing and education in the Mid-West, raising three children along the way and then moving with his Wisconsin-born wife to Florida (isn't that what you do after tiring of cold northern winters?), Randy has been pursuing his passion as an author and motivational speaker for over a decade. Randy is the guy you want to talk to if you are having a bad day because his infectious enthusiasm and booming voice will surely brighten your spirits. His sharp communication skills, sensitivity to an audience and mastery of turning any topic into something interesting is both a skill and art.

In search of diverse feedback, my good friend **Brian Schober** always takes an interest in my hobbies, so he quickly signed up to read the manuscript. Brian is a Navy veteran, aviation pilot and systems engineer supporting the US defense industry, working for a global SPM service company. A former Lockheed Martin manager and now leading large, distributed teams for an independent contracting firm, Brian provided valuable input on the relationships between managers and front-line employees. **Michele Evans**, a former member of my team at Microsoft, has been a leader of people teams at Facebook/Meta and now an entrepreneur with her own coaching and mentoring start-up.

Because of her warm personality, sense of humor, optimistic outlook and eye for detail on many of our shared experiences at Microsoft, Michele has been a valued contributor to the final product now in your hands. And my thanks to **Cliff Martin**, a long-time friend whose family of origin had a similar experience as the Hansons in our story, on a smaller scale. His guidance helped make their "story" come alive.

You must know by now that I am a big fan of finding the right partners on any project we may be undertaking. **Trevor Fox**, who helped me with a variety of editorial services on my first book, *Significant* (self-published under the Kindle Publishing imprint) was also a valued contributor to this work of *Stakeholders*. Keenly in tune with a structural vision of how content gets knitted and pieced together, Trevor was also helpful in helping me define the audience and speak with realism and authenticity to an audience of learners. Also, **Eli Creasy**, an artist by training, was a key contributor to *Stakeholders* with illustrations, visual charts and tables, and suggestions for a few additions that are pleasing to the eye.

I am so grateful for the team at Collective Ink Business Books for partnering with me to edit, market, produce and distribute *Stakeholders* to a wide audience of prospective readers. My special thanks to **Vicky Hartley** and **Frank Smecker** who ran point on the project, **Gavin Davies** who provided valuable insights into content revisions, marketing strategy and distribution and copy-editor **Sarah Hodder** who gently corrected my use of punctuation.

You may have also noticed that a number of talented professionals were kind to read the manuscript and share their endorsement of the book with prospective readers. I sincerely appreciate their acknowledgement of the value of this work, and willingness to share their stamp of approval.

Carol Englizian is my loving spouse and constant cheerleader in all personal and professional pursuits. We are senior members of an extended family of about 40 people, and they are to a fault incredibly supportive of my writing and the purpose it gives me. I love and adore each of you and thank you for the encouragement to keep writing.

One of the more common pieces of feedback I heard in the evolution of this writing project was how much readers enjoyed the story of Hanson's Home & Hardware. Some of the early readers even doubted my assertion that Hanson is fiction. They wanted to hear a big reveal, so here it is. The Hanson's story **is** fictional and is woven from my personal interactions with a few key influences like these:

- The Martin family from Albany, Oregon did in fact have a similar story of their early years starting a successful fire suppression-system business, but the extent of their service area did not expand beyond their home state.
- Having lived on two occasions in the state of Illinois, I am familiar with many of the names and places used to bring realism into the Hanson's story.
- Details of the Hanson's story was enriched by my early career experiences in the hospitality industry (my first business "lemonade-stand" learning lab) and later at the national retailer Walgreens, where we encountered many of the same challenges faced by Ted and his team.
- The examples of labor cost, workers compensation claims, inventory loss and even the management training investment are true episodes from my exposure to these dynamic business issues as a corporate leader with multiple employers.

Not long after I joined Microsoft, we began a personal and professional association with Henry and Debbie Brown and the Laird Norton Company, a family office that supports multiple generations of legacy-connected investors. Serving as an adviser to LNC for over 20 years, my connections with former CEO, Jeff Vincent, current CEO, Brian McGuigan, and board members including Steve Clifford, Joe Williams, Lisa Brummel, Laura Jennings, Debbie Brown and Bill Lewis gave me incredible insight into the world of venture capital, financial stewardship, entrepreneurship and business start-ups. One unexpected connection that came out of this engagement was an invitation to speak to the Family Business Network, where I met Andrew Keyt who at the time was the Executive Director of the Family Business Center at Loyola University of Chicago. These relationships, and what I learned from connecting with the LNC and FBN leaders were incredibly helpful to me as the creation of the Hanson's story became an important piece in the development of the content for *Stakeholders*.

Feedback from early readers is also consistent regarding the value of the real-life anecdotes included in the book. While some have requested more detail on a few of the stories, it has been my contention that not every reader has an appetite for this; and it is important that we not get distracted from the primary themes of the book that need to efficiently build one upon another, at a pace that fits the reading style of more people.

The story about my interaction with Amazon CEO Jeff Bezos about the employee time-off benefit has attracted interest from more than a few readers. A few contextual details are important, such as this conversation with Jeff was early in my tenure, it was conducted over email and there was quite a bit of back-and-forth. I knew quite early in my role at Amazon that Jeff had a conviction about one-way and two-way doors.[1]

Jeff viewed the introduction or expansion of an employee benefit as a one-way door, in the sense that once offered, the company would never unwind the decision — at the risk of severely damaging the company's reputation with the workforce. He simply wanted me to be thorough in the logic of my proposal and that we had contemplated all the intended and unintended consequences of what we were considering.

Now before you get testy at the idea that leaders may see an employee benefit as a one-way door, it does happen to be supported by history. For example, defined-benefit pension plans were a staple of the employment value proposition at many large US companies prior to the 1980s when it was reported that 38% of private sector employees were covered under such a plan. Going back more than a century to its introduction in 1875, the American Express Company offered employees a defined benefit pension plan which guaranteed a monthly amount of income for life — calculated by a formula based on earnings and years of service.[2]

The problem is, and Bezos knew this, many company pension plans were underfunded, not unlike the social security income plan offered since the 1930s by the US Federal Government. So, these employers took unprecedented action to freeze benefits, close the port of entry to new employees and look for substitutes that were fiscally less expensive. This eventually led to the prominence of defined contribution plans that shifted funding to the employee, with only a modest subsidy by the employer. From the perspective of the company and its shareholders, this was a necessary trade-off, but is also a classic case of competing stakeholder agendas that made roadkill of employees counting on annuitized pension plan income at retirement.

Other pre-release readers I called upon were unaware that Microsoft had changed how it granted company stock to employees. When the company was formed by Bill Gates and Paul Allen, they owned 100% of the firm. Eventually, in exchange for an infusion of cash, one venture capital partner received a small ownership stake, and then later Bill and Paul diluted their share when Steve Ballmer joined up and was granted a percentage of ownership in the company.[3] (Just to put that in context, for every $1000 in value at the time Steve joined up with Bill and Paul would now — as of May 2024 — yield a value of $5.9 million).

When the company went public in 1986, it also began offering non-qualified stock options to executives and all professional employees (a large majority of the total workforce). As the company catapulted onto the technology scene and became the #1 software provider globally, the value of these stock options grew exponentially creating a large crowd of instant employee-millionaires. Many were barely a few years away from the university campus, and now they had life-changing wealth. Some decided to leave Microsoft and launch new ventures, others began investing in start-ups and new technology, and others stayed at Microsoft to focus on changing the desktop experience forever. The highest-paid employees who stayed and kept accumulating even more wealth are reverently referred to as "volunteers."

A stock compensation crisis occurred just months into the new century, when the value of Microsoft stock declined rapidly due to a variety of business and regulatory factors. It was this panic that caused Steve Ballmer to noodle on a few possible remedies with our team, including double-digit salary increases and matching stock grants. The emotions connected to the promise of generational wealth for new and existing employees continued to run hot until late in 2002 when we began to look seriously at substituting the practice of granting restricted stock units for the legacy practice of granting stock options. In case you are unfamiliar with these compensation instruments, a stock option gives the employee value only when two things occur: (1) the employee is still at the company after the vesting (waiting) period; and (2) the fair market value of the stock (on Wall Street) is higher than it was on the date the option shares were granted. Because Microsoft stock value was dropping rather than rising, thousands of employees held option shares that were worthless to them unless they cared to hang around for ten years (the life of the option) and hoped fortunes would change. By contrast, restricted stock units are full shares of company stock whose value rises and falls according to the fair market value on Wall Street. The only downsides are the recipient is granted fewer shares than options (due to the difference in value), and the time restriction placed on access to the shares usually requires months or years of continued employment. You see, when fair market value falls and a stock option is worthless, the restricted stock unit (RSU) always has value — even if you must wait to get your hands on the shares.

After months of analysis, modeling, and "war room" sessions where we remained in front of our laptops from sunrise to sunset, we finally had a proposal that went to the SLT (senior leadership team). Our proposal had many advantages over the current practice of granting stock options; however, it meant stepping away from a practice that had become legendary within the company's culture. Using his top-to-top connections in financial services, Steve Ballmer lined up a banking partner who was willing to take on transfers of "out of the money", unexercised stock options held by employees in exchange for a cash settlement worth "pennies on the dollar." The SLT suggested that before granting final approval, we should carefully study how this change would impact the competitiveness of our employee compensation package.

I was tasked personally with the research to predict how the change in "realized compensation" would impact our ability to attract and retain the best talent in the industry. I worked with my direct boss and the head of HR to clear everything off my calendar for two weeks, and the project became my "24/7 everything." Reaching out to industry contacts, pouring over survey data, interviewing Microsoft employees who came from other highly respected technology employers, and applying my training and experience I was able to condense my findings into a 40-page white paper that was directly submitted to the founder of the company. Bill Gates read the report and sent word to the SLT that it was the finest white paper he had seen from the HR function at Microsoft, and he weighed in to support the proposed change. While that was extremely gratifying to hear, I was soon thereafter humbled by an executive who wanted to know the identity of the outside consultant who created such a fine report, because it surely could not have been Mark Englizian. How do I feel about that insult? It's simply a nod to the cruelty that we sometimes experience in the corporate world.

In this final example of expanding story details, I promise to be more succinct. The Walgreens profit-sharing design proposal we offered to the leadership did a very simple thing. Instead of calculating a profit-sharing pool for distribution to employee retirement accounts that was a fixed percentage of net profit, I proposed we set a floor of profitability equal to the fiscal plan approved by the board of directors. At a high level, assume the fiscal plan for the year was $50 billion in revenue and $1.5 billion of net profit. The old formula would calculate profit-sharing as a percentage of $1.5 billion, while the new approach mandated that the company generate at least $1.5 billion of net profit **before any** profit-sharing would be distributed. Since the contract negotiations with Express Scripts broke down after the fiscal plan was approved, and the profit shortfall was expected to be significant, the proposed modification would then pay out $0 in profit share distributions. What sold the plan to executives was an expected immediate savings of $80 million, and what sold the plan to employees was the temporary impact of this formula shift and that we modified the upside above the profit plan target to create the prospect of more generous profit-sharing distributions than had been experienced in prior years.

Mark Englizian
July, 2024

Citations and Sources

Introduction

1. Bill George and David Gergen, *Discover Your True North*, (Jossey-Bass, 2015).

Chapter One: Case Study

1. Nitin Nohria, "What the Case Study Method Really Teaches," in *Harvard Business Publishing,* December 21, 2021, https://hbsp.harvard.edu/inspiring-minds.
2. Harvard Business Review case studies, https://store.hbr.org/case-studies.

Chapter Two: Money Matters

1. Brian Tracy, "The Basics of Business Success," in *Entrepreneur,* April 18, 2005, https://www.entrepreneur.com/starting-a-business.

Chapter Three: People Groups

1. Ima Robot, "Greenback Boogie," *Another Man's Treasure*, Werewolf Heart Records, 2010.
2. Richard Meade, "Suez blockage extends as salvors fail to free Ever Given," in *Lloyd's List,* March 25, 2021, https://lloydslist.com.

3. Statista Research Department, "Number of frontline workers in the United States in 2020, by industry," in *Statista*, February 2, 2024, https://www.statista.com/statistics.
4. Statista Research Department, "Number of part-time employees in the United States from 1990 to 2023," in *Statista*, February 15, 2024, https://www.statista.com/statistics.
5. The Conference Board index of consumer confidence, https://www.conference-board.org/topics/consumer-confidence.

Chapter Four: Competing Interests

1. Illustration titled "Understanding Conflict in the Workplace," Work Wellness Institute, http://workwellnessinstitute.org.
2. Ian Webster, "Stock market returns between 1982 and 1992," *S&P 500 Data (Official Data Foundation)*, https://www.officialdata.org/us/stocks/s-p-500/1982.
3. Paolo Confino, "Australian winemaker just paid $1 billion for a California vineyard owned by two brothers who started making wine in their garage," in *Fortune*, October 31, 2023, https://fortune.com.
4. Jen Fisher and Paul H. Silverglate, "The C-suite's role in well-being," in *Deloitte Insights*, June 22, 2022, https://www2.deloitte.com/us.
5. Yuval Noah Harari, *Homo Deus: A Brief History of Tomorrow*, (Harvill Secker, 2016).
6. Ryan Phillips, "Stephen Strasburg's Contract is Undoubtedly the Worst in Sports History," in *The Big Lead*, August 26, 2023, https://www.thebiglead.com/posts/stephen-strasburg.

7. Jesse Dougherty and Barry Sevruga, "Stephen Strasburg, the Nat's' World Series MVP, plans to retire," in *The Washington Post*, August 24, 2023, https://www.washingtonpost.com/sports.
8. Josh Benjamin, "Agents Like Scott Boras Are Ruining the Sport of Baseball," in *Bleacher Report*, February 1, 2012, https://bleacherreport.com.
9. Steve Clifford, *The CEO Pay Machine: How it Trashes America and How to Stop It*, (Blue Rider Press, 2017).
10. Josh Bivens and Jori Kandra, "CEO pay has skyrocketed 1,460% since 1978," in *Economic Policy Institute*, October 4, 2022, https://www.epi.org.
11. Ellen Huet, "Silicon Valley's Quest to Live Forever Has Many Warring Factions," in *Bloomberg*, December 19, 2023, https://www.bloomberg.com.
12. Former Enron Chief Executive Officer Jeffrey Skilling Sentenced to More Than 24 Years in Prison on Fraud, Conspiracy Charges, *US Department of Justice*, October 23, 2006, https://www.justice.gov/archive.
13. Adam Hayes, "Bernie Madoff: Who He Was, How His Ponzi Scheme Worked," in *Investopedia*, updated December 20, 2023, https://www.investopedia.com.
14. Elizabeth Holmes Profile, in *Forbes*, accessed April 5, 2024, https://www.forbes.com/profile/elizabeth-holmes.
15. Nicholas Biase, "Trevor Milton Sentenced to Four Years in Prison For Securities Fraud Scheme," *U.S. Attorney's Office, Southern District of New York*, December 18, 2023, https://www.justice.gov/usao-sdny/pr.
16. Luc Cohen and Jody Godoy, "Bankman-Fried sentenced to 25 years for multi-billion dollar FTX fraud," in *Reuters*, March 28, 2024, https://www.reuters.com/technology.
17. "The Giving Pledge," https://givingpledge.org.

18. Luisa Zhou, "The Percentage of Businesses That Fail (Statistics & Failure Rates)," in *Zhou Ventures*, updated July 28, 2023, https://www.luisazhou.com/blog.
19. Amazon and Hyundai launch a broad, strategic partnership — including vehicle sales on Amazon.com in 2024, in *Amazon News*, November 16, 2023, https://www.aboutamazon.com/news.
20. Associated Press, "Internet provider buying Excite, At Home's $6.7 billion deal among largest by communications firm," in *Deseret News*, January 19, 1999, https://www.deseret.com.
21. Wikipedia contributors, "@Home Network," *Wikipedia, The Free Encyclopedia*, accessed April 5, 2024, https://en.wikipedia.org.
22. Jacob Greenspon, "How Big a Problem Is It That a Few Shareholders Own Stock in So Many Competing Companies?" in *Harvard Business Review*, updated February 22, 2019, https://hbr.org/2019/02.

Chapter Five: Survive and Thrive

1. Packard, Dave. "Supervisory Development Program" HP, Palo Alto, CA, March 8, 1960.
2. Frank Olio and Alex Bitter, "Blockbuster: The rise and fall of the movie rental store, and what happened to the brand," in *Business Insider*, April 24, 2023, https://www.businessinsider.com.
3. Associated Press, "Borders books to close, along with 10,700 jobs," *CBS News*, July 18, 2011, https://www.cbsnews.com/news.
4. Mark Hall, "Compaq," in *Britannica Money*, Updated April 1, 2024, https://www.britannica.com/money/Compaq.

5. "After 60 years, Polaroid quits instant film business," in *The Economic Times*, February 9, 2008, https://economictimes.indiatimes.com.
6. Nick Routley, "Internet Browser Market Share (1996 – 2019)," in *Visual Capitalist*, January 20, 2020, https://www.visualcapitalist.com.
7. Henry R. Norr, "Netscape Communications Corp." in *Britannica Money*, updated February 29, 2024, https://www.britannica.com/money.
8. Jeremy Goldman, "13 Insightful Quotes from Intel Visionary Andy Grove," *Inc.com*, March 21, 2016, https://www.inc.com/jeremy-goldman/13-insightful-quotes-from-intel-visionary-andy-grove.html.
9. Truman Du, "Animation: The Largest Public Companies by Market Cap (2000–2022)," in *Visual Capitalist*, October 17, 2022, https://www.visualcapitalist.com.
10. Apple Inc., "'Apple Park' Design, History & Facts: $5 Billion Apple's Cupertino HQ," *IFuture*, January 16, 2023, https://apple-store.ifuture.co.in/blog.
11. "Plan Your Visit," *Sofi* Stadium, accessed April 10, 2024, https://www.sofistadium.com.
12. Matt Krantz, "13 S&P 500 Dividend Stocks Pay 50% More Than 10-Year Treasuries," in *Investor's Business Daily*, December 7, 2023, https://www.investors.com.
13. "Our History," *CVS Health, accessed April 10, 2024*, https://www.cvshealth.com/about/our-strategy/company-history.
14. Bruce Jaspen, "CVS Health Profits Hit $2 Billion As Company Benefits from Obamacare and New Businesses," in *Forbes*, February 7, 2024, https://www.forbes.com/sites.
15. "CVS Health Corp. Investor Day" (Boston, MA, December 5, 2023), FactSet Call Street.

Chapter Six: Intersection Chaos

1. Karen Martin, "The Company Chaos You Don't Know You're Creating," in *Fast Company,* July 6, 2012, https://www.fastcompany.com.
2. Larry Fink, "Larry Fink's 2022 Letter to CEOs: The Power of Capitalism," in *BlackRock,* 2022, https://www.blackrock.com/us.
3. Emily Le Coz, "Prescription for disaster: America's broken pharmacy system in revolt over burnout and errors," in *USA Today*, October 26, 2023, https://www.usatoday.com.
4. Lauren Rosenblatt, Seattle Times, "'The only enemy is Amazon': Chris Smalls talks Bezos, unions during WA visit," in *The Spokesman-Review*, July 19, 2023, https://www.spokesman.com.
5. Paul Roberts, "PCC and its workers still paying for pandemic and years of ambitious expansion," in *The Seattle Times,* October 26, 2023, https://www.seattletimes.com/business.
6. Kshama Sawant, "Why I'm Not Running Again for City Council," in *The Stranger,* January 19, 2023, https://www.thestranger.com/guest-editorial.
7. Jon Talton, "How Billionaires are Changing Seattle and America for better and worse," in *The Seattle Times*, November 17, 2023, https://www.seattletimes.com/business.
8. Jenn Hardy, Office of Assembly Majority Leader Emerita Eloise Gómez Reyes, "Assembly member Reyes Responds to Amazon's Leaked Community Engagement Plan," in *California State Assembly Democratic Caucus*, December 5, 2023, https://a50.asmdc.org.

Chapter Seven: Priorities

1. Kristi Coulter, *Exit Interview: The Life and Death of My Ambitious Career*, (MCD Books, 2023).
2. Thomas J. Saporito, "It's Time to Acknowledge CEO Loneliness," in *Harvard Business Review*, February 5, 2012, https://hbr.org.
3. David Gelles, "Billionaire No More: Patagonia Founder Gives Away the Company," in *The New York Times*, September 14, 2022, https://www.nytimes.com.
4. Sam Walton and John Huey, *Sam Walton: Made in America*, (Doubleday, 1992; Bantam Books, 2012 reissue).
5. Leah Goldman, "WALMART: How the Tiny Little Mom and Pop Shop Became a Billion-Dollar Business," in *Business Insider*, February 3, 2011, https://www.businessinsider.com.
6. Legere, John, "T-Mobile's Legere Refers to AT&T and Verizon as 'Dumb and Dumber'." Interview by Vonnie Quinn, Bloomberg Television. February 8, 2018. Video, 2:52. https://youtube.com.
7. Richard Feloni, "T-Mobile's CEO tells young people he 'can summarize everything you need to know to lead a major corporation' with 2 pieces of advice," in *Business Insider*, October 12, 2016, https://www.businessinsider.com.
8. Tim Barber, "Brands must take advantage of Twitter's personal touch," in *The Guardian*, February 24, 2015, https://www.theguardian.com.
9. "Kenneth H. Blanchard Quotes," in *Goodreads*, accessed April 19, 2024, https://www.goodreads.com/author/quotes.

Chapter Eight: Affordability of Investing in People

1. Proverbs 30:7–9, New International Version of the Bible.
2. "CEO Job Description," *CEO Search*, accessed April 13, 2024, https://www.ceo-search.com/ceo-job-description.
3. "Amazon.com Announces Record Free Cash Flow Fueled by Lower Prices and Free Shipping; Introduces New Express Shipping Program — Amazon Prime," *Amazon Press Center*, accessed April 13, 2024, https://press.aboutamazon.com/2005.
4. Daniel Howley, "Amazon Prime now has 200 million members, jumping 50 million in one year," in *Yahoo! Finance* April 15, 2021, https://finance.yahoo.com/news.
5. "The Amazon Prime Membership Fee," *Amazon.com*, accessed April 13, 2024, https://www.amazon.com/gp/help/customer.

Chapter Nine: Repurposing Legacy Investments

1. Hamel, Gary, November 1, 2021. Cartoon. https://www.garyhamel.com/humor.
2. Knight, Phil, "The David Rubenstein Show: Phil Knight." Interview by David Rubenstein, *Bloomberg*, June 28, 2017. Video, 24:24. https://www.bloomberg.com/news/videos.

Chapter Ten: Modernizing for Asset Efficiency

1. "Singapore country profile," *BBC News*, September 4, 2023, https://www.bbc.com/news.
2. Wikipedia contributors, "Singapore," *Wikipedia, The Free Encyclopedia*, accessed April 14, 2024, https://en.wikipedia.org/wiki/Singapore.

Chapter Eleven: Use It or Lose It

1. Paraphrased from Matt. 25:14–25, The Message Bible.

Chapter Twelve: Decision Time

1. "Laxman Narasimhan Assumes Role of Starbucks Chief Executive Officer," *Starbucks Stories & News,* March 20, 2023, https://stories.starbucks.com/press.
2. "Microsoft Acquires Navision," announced July 11, 2002, https://news.microsoft.com.
3. Sean Williams, "If You Invested $10,000 in Amazon for Its IPO in 1997, Here's How Much You'd Have Now," in *The Motley Fool,* September 22, 2022, https://www.fool.com/investing.
4. "Our History," *Walgreen Co.,* accessed April 13, 2024, https://www.walgreens.com/topic/about/companyhistory.
5. Jim Collins, *Good to Great: Why Some Companies Make the Leap ... And Others Don't,* (Harper Collins Publishers, 2001).
6. Bruce Jaspen, "Walgreen and Express Scripts Reach Deal," in *The New York Times,* July 19, 2012, https://www.nytimes.com.

Chapter Thirteen: The Sauce

1. Brooks, David, *How to Know a Person: The Art of Seeing Others Deeply and Being Deeply Seen,* (Random House, 2023).
2. Dictionary.com, "Secret sauce," accessed April 13, 2024, https://www.dictionary.com.

3. "Resources," *Rob Cross*, https://www.robcross.org/resources.
4. Mary Barra, *Autoline This Week* interview, October 12, 2012.
5. Alexa Mikhail, "From Brian Chesky and Tim Cook to the Founder of Toms Shoes, It's Lonely at the Top", in *Fortune* Magazine, May 28, 2024 (interview with Ryan Jenkins).
6. Richard Feloni, "The T-Mobile CEO who calls his competition 'dumb and dumber' explains how he doubled customers in 4 years, and how a group of employees made him cry," in *Business Insider*, October 7, 2016, https://www.businessinsider.com.
7. Nicole Heimann, "Courageous Leadership: Why CEOs Should Take a Stand," in *Forbes*, June 22, 2023, https://www.forbes.com.
8. Rich Dec, "Is Your CEO Courageous?" *Great Place to Work,* May 14, 2015, https://www.greatplacetowork.com/resources/blog.
9. Jennifer Pellet, "Courage: One of 11 CEO Leadership Qualities," in *Chief Executive,* accessed January 31, 2024, https://chiefexecutive.net.
10. Anna Wilde Mathews, "Walgreens Earnings Beat Forecasts; New CEO Slashes Dividend," in *The Wall Street Journal,* January 4, 2024, https://www.wsj.com.
11. Douglas Conant, "Doug Conant: CEOs Must Find Their Courage," in *Chief Executive,* accessed April 13, 2024, https://chiefexecutive.net.

Chapter Fourteen: A New Personal Ethos

1. Adam Grant, https://www.threads.net/@adamgrant/post.

2. Oprah Winfrey, https://www.passiton.com/inspirational-quotes.

Author Notes and Acknowledgements

1. Colin Bryar and Bill Carr, *Working Backwards — Insights, Stories and Secrets from Inside Amazon*, (St. Martin's Press, 2021).
2. Investopedia, https://www.investopedia.com/terms/p/pensionplan.
3. Ben Gilbert and David Rosenthal, "Acquired" podcast, April 21, 2024, Microsoft: The Complete History and Strategy (acquired.fm).

BUSINESS
BOOKS

Business Books

Business Books publishes practical guides
and insightful non-fiction for beginners and professionals.
Covering aspects from management skills, leadership and
organizational change to positive work environments, career
coaching and self-care for managers, our books are a valuable
addition to those working in the world of business.

Recent Bestsellers from Business Books Are:

From 50 to 500
Jonathan Dapra, Richard Dapra and Jonas Akerman
An engaging and innovative small business leadership framework guaranteed to strengthen a leader's effectiveness to drive company growth and results.
Paperback: 978-1-78904-743-1 ebook: 978-1-78904-744-8

Be Visionary
Marty Strong
Be Visionary: Strategic Leadership in the Age of Optimization
Demonstrates to existing and aspiring leaders the positive impact of applying visionary creativity and decisiveness to achieve spectacular long-range results while balancing the day-to-day.
Paperback: 978-1-78535-432-8 ebook: 978-1-78535-433-5

Finding Sustainability
Trent A. Romer
Journey to eight states, three national parks and three countries to experience the life-changing education that led Trent A. Romer to find sustainability for his plastic-bag manufacturing business and himself.
Paperback: 978-1-78904-601-4 ebook: 978-1-78904-602-1

Inner Brilliance, Outer Shine
Estelle Read
Optimise your success, performance, productivity and well-being to lead your best business life.
Paperback: 978-1-78904-803-2 ebook: 978-1-78904-804-9

Tomorrow's Jobs Today
Rafael Moscatel and Abby Jane Moscatel
Discover leadership secrets and technology strategies being pioneered by today's most innovative business executives and renowned brands across the globe.
Paperback: 978-1-78904-561-1 ebook: 978-1-78904-562-8

Secrets to Successful Property Investment
Deb Durbin
Your complete guide to building a property portfolio.
Paperback: 978-1-78904-818-6 ebook: 978-1-78904-819-3

The Effective Presenter
Ryan Warriner
The playbook to professional presentation success!
Paperback: 978-1-78904-795-0 ebook: 978-1-78904-796-7

The Beginner's Guide to Managing
Mikil Taylor
A how-to guide for first-time managers adjusting to their new leadership roles.
Paperback: 978-1-78904-583-3 ebook: 978-1-78904-584-0

Forward
Elizabeth Moran
A practical playbook for leaders to guide their teams through their organization's next big change.
Paperback: 978-1-78279-289-5 ebook: 978-1-78279-291-8

Readers of ebooks can buy or view any of these bestsellers by clicking on the live link in the title. Most titles are published in paperback and as an ebook. Paperbacks are available in traditional bookshops. Both print and ebook formats are available online.

Find more titles and sign up to our readers' newsletter at www.collectiveinkbooks.com/business-books